GROCK

LIFE'S A LARK

GROCK
LIFE'S A LARK

By

GROCK

LONDON
WILLIAM HEINEMANN LTD

TRANSLATED FROM THE GERMAN
BY MADGE PEMBERTON
EDITED BY EDUARD BEHRENS

FIRST PUBLISHED 1931
PRINTED IN GREAT BRITAIN
AT THE WINDMILL PRESS

CONTENTS

v

CONTENTS

ILLUSTRATIONS

ILLUSTRATIONS

A ROYAL CONFINEMENT

Grock, the greatest clown in all the world!
How the hoardings shriek it at you from
every street and public place the world over.
My name gleams, large as life, above the
Variety Theatre. All the streets and houses
are ablaze with it so soon as it is night, while
the little birds wake up and carol in the
gardens, thinking it is day. Aeronauts,
dazzled by the shine of it, are misled as to
their landing stage. In fact the roof of the
music-hall, while I am playing beneath it,
may be said to be turned into a landing stage
for aeroplanes . . .

Not that any of this bombast is really *me*.
Grock, as a matter of fact, is not Grock at
all. To my very excellent backers, managers
and publicity agents must be ascribed this
house of entertainment with my name in
flames of fire.

GROCK

As for the Grock who is *not* Grock, he smokes forty cigarettes a day, drinks his glass of beer, wears patent underclothes and wants nothing so much as a little peace and quiet. Such a very little quiet and peace. He would like to be left to hoe his patch of potatoes, sow his spinach and plant his cherries. He is as homely as were his beginnings.

Father and Mother lived in Reconvilier, a little Swiss village of peasants and watchmakers in the Berner Jura. They had inherited my grandfather's little workshop. The Berner Jura is one of those new-fangled cantonal districts where they speak French.

But my grandparents derived from the old German portion of it and my grandfather spoke only "Bärndütsch."

For the natives of Berne, "Bärndütsch" is the loveliest language upon earth. I must admit I find a little of it goes a long way.

Christian, or Chrigu, as the Bernese have it, the old manservant in my grandfather's house, had a spouse, Eisi, or Elsa, a regular whopper of a woman. Whenever Chrigu was in a tender frame of mind, he would first remove with finger and thumb all the scraps of shag tobacco from the interstices of his cheek, laying them down to dry in front of the oven or on the window sill after which he would spit and wipe his mouth, and holding out his bristly countenance, emit the following guttural command: "Give us a buss, Eisi wench . . . give us a good smacking 'un on the chops . . ."

And Eisi would waddle up to him forthwith, and give him one that really *was* a good smacking'un, and sounded like nothing so much as—no . . . I'll not say it . . .

But that is *Bärndütsch*.

Grandfather died at the age of seventy-six, from a poisoned cut, the result of trying to extract a corn. He would have approved of Michael Angelo, who never took his boots off for three years on end, or so they say. My belief is that grandfather would never have taken *his* off all his life, if he hadn't been plagued by corns. The brook flowed in front of our house, fresh and inviting. But to bathe his feet in it grandfather would have had to go down at least five steps. Couldn't be done. Added to which, he hated water like poison.

His voice was rough and scratchy as a

scrubbing-brush. I can hear him now, calling out:

"You boy, Adrien, get me a nip o' tater-grog and bring it home-along!"

On which off I would speed to the public-house and purchase a peg of potato brandy. One day I succumbed to temptation and tasted it. But the next moment I had spat out the hellish brew, and all but spilled the rest out of the mug in my horror. I made haste to fill it up again with water from the fountain. But grandfather snuffed it in a twink:

"You rascally urchin you—you've watered it!"

With a look of loathing that I'll never forget, he hurled the mug into the dust-bin. That is how best I remember grandfather.

As for grandmother, the cows in her stable were the greatest pride and joy of her life. I verily believe that, had she been able, she would have fed them from marble mangers, and littered them with feather-beds. She would collect remnants of wadding from the village tailors and wipe with them her darlings' backsides. I can see her now, spectacles on nose, a cow's tail uplifted in

one hand and a piece of wadding in the other. She rejoiced in paying such delicate attentions to the apples of her eye.

Being brought up from childhood in the Berner Jura, my father became a perfect French Swiss, and took to wife just such another. My mother hailed from Neuchâtel, and could count a certain ancestry to her credit, for she came of Huguenot stock that had fled to Switzerland from the horrors of St. Bartholomew. My ancestor rejoiced in the name of Daguet Monte à Cheval.

I was the product of a most tender mother and a stout, intrepid father. My father could wield a pitchfork, second to none, but this did not prevent him from being one of the most cunning artificers of intricate ladies' watches. He was passionately fond of shooting and wrestling, and was constantly winning the best local prizes for these sports all round the neighbourhood. Indeed, for fourteen years, his was the pride of place among wrestlers.

Even to-day, when I visit the Jura villages I am liable to be buttonholed by aged cronies betwixt Bienne and La Chaux-de-Fonds, who draw me on one side and vaunt my father's praises: "Adolf Wettach...ah ... now he *was* a man ..."

Which is precisely what he was. Whosoever took it into his head to insult him would soon find himself lying flat on his back in the next street without much knowledge how he got there.

"I would rather keep guard over a sack of fleas than bring up Adolf." So said my grandmother.

When he was sixteen, he vanished from the household without a word of warning. Grandmother, with her usual promptitude, ran to the police. And where do you suppose they found the delinquent? An hour's journey away, in the town of Bienne, in the midst of rehearsing an acrobatic turn with Marinelli's travelling circus.

My mother, too, just before I was born, had an experience by no means without its significance. A sports' contest was being held at Tavannes, the chief village of the valley. My father, as a leading light of the Committee, would go over every evening, returning by the last train. A neighbour called on my mother with the cryptic words: "If you want to see something strange, go to the first

7   B

performance of the circus that is being given at Tavannes."

"Why, what should I see there?" my mother asked.

"Your husband."

In spite of being so near her time, my mother hastened straightaway and bought a ticket for the front row.

The circus was an old friend to all the Bienne population. It belonged no more to Marinelli, but to his son-in-law, Ricono. Ricono had become an intimate friend of my father, and I think it must have been the latter's popularity throughout the country-side that caused the circus-proprietor to set up his tent in Tavannes.

At any rate the booth was crowded with villagers from all parts. The performance began, numbers one, two and three came and went, and then number four, the star turn that was to be a flying-trapeze and slack-wire act. And lo and behold! there stood my father in the midst of the troupe! There he was, hanging on to the trapeze, making a prodigious swing, preparatory to balancing himself on his rope. But just as he was about to seize hold of his balancing pole, his glance

8

fell on my mother's upturned face.

"Call yourself my husband ... aren't you ashamed of yourself?"

So loud did she shout that the whole audience turned to look at her. You could have heard a pin drop. Then, with his balancing pole under his arm, my father slithered down the rope, laid the pole, without a word, down by the footlights, and stole out of the tent, his tail between his legs.

Four days later on the 10th of January, 1880, I came into the world. Now I ask you, is it altogether by chance that I was born a mountebank?

So much for father.

Twenty-eight years later another lady was obliged to hasten away from a circus owing to the dictates of nature. This time the lady was a Queen—the Queen of Spain.

Antonet, my dear old friend, Antonet, sharer of all my Spanish triumphs, do you still remember the Parish Circus in Madrid, all those years ago? Four thousand pairs of eyes were staring at us. Two pairs belonged to the King and the Queen. The King sat, leaning over the edge of the Royal Box, his Hapsburgian chin cupped in his hand.

The number in question was called "Serenade for Marietta." You came in first with your violin under your arm, dragging a chair after you on which you sat and then began to play a soulful melody, looking round admiringly for universal applause. But the hand-clapping ended as soon as it had begun, for forthwith I made my entrance with my pink, round head, bald as a billiard ball, and my face like a sucking-pig, complete with chair, grin, cow-bell and drum. The audience roared. At me.

On which you stop short, furious, and lay down your fiddle. Cool as a cucumber, I sit myself down on my chair, proceeding to ring my cow-bell, beat my drum and croak my song.

"Get up, you rapscallion! Can't you see I'm singing a serenade to my sweetheart?"

I beat my drum, and croak my song to a *decrescendo* before I reply: "With your permission I too wish to serenade my sweetheart!"

Further business with bell and drum, to the accompaniment of my voice, all very loud.

"Will you get up?"

11

You rise from your seat and make towards me with threatening gestures. So terrified am I, I get into a panic, beating my drum so frenziedly that it bursts, and hey presto! I fall through it, bell and all, head first.

"Must be an odd sort of sweetheart to like to be serenaded with cow-bells ..."

On which I stick my head pathetically through the drum-opening, and make my excuse:

"Oh! lots of 'em, believe me ..."

It was at this point that the Royal Box could contain itself no longer. Four and twenty hours later a Spanish Infanta saw the light. The Queen's laughter had been too much for her; she had gone straight from the circus to childbed.

So you see that wheresoever Grock antics the stork is never far away.

2

ADVENTURE WITH THE ORIENT EXPRESS

AND now to work. The slippery rope of the author's craft has yet to be climbed, the dizziest and most coveted of all far-away peaks to be attained. Shall I pull off this trick as I have pulled off many another? Never was I more ardent for applause.

This year finds me with professional engagements all over Europe, starting with Marseilles. I have dates in the following order: Paris, Düsseldorf, Berlin, Nuremberg, Budapest, Hamburg, Amsterdam, Frankfort, London, Geneva, Vienna, Hanover, Münster in Westphalia.

I start writing in my dressing-room at Marseilles. I shall always write in my dressing-room, where I feel at ease—spiritually in my shirt-sleeves, so to say. Here, if anywhere, I fancy I can make the hotch-potch of my life into something like a palatable mixture.

Well then, the world weighed the heavier

by ten lbs., and bore upon its surface one yowling baby the more. Even as an infant in arms, I soon started to prove I was cut to no ordinary measure, as evidenced by my insatiable hunger coupled with my digestive capacity. The whole household was soon mobilised to attend to my infantile requirements. For a whole year the yard outside our house was white with baby linen hanging up to dry. We became the superstition of the neighbourhood. Carters avoided our street because their horses shied at it, and tales went abroad of battalions of white-winged angels a-flutter above our chimney pots at night time.

When I was three, my people moved to Neuveville by the Lake of Bienne. I remember I wore red knickerbockers and a cap with a tassel.

Our house in Neuveville was quite close to the station, and my favourite playground was the railway line where the great trains would rush through on their way to Constantinople, Vienna, Zürich, Paris, past the shores of the lake. Other children were content with a nodding acquaintance from the fastness of their front gardens. But this wasn't good enough for baby Grock, who from the very first moment felt an affinity towards the International Train Service. One fine day found me playing, trustful as Daniel in the lions' den, between the lines, with the gigantic Orient Express thundering towards me. On it came, roaring in a welter of steam. The whistle screamed, and I started to run, but the tail of my coat got caught in one of the rails. If a rescuing fist hadn't clutched me that instant minute, the world would have had to get on as best it might without a Grock. Fancy the world without Grock—old Grock, with his lemons and rum! Scarce conceivable, is it? But the station-master saved it from such a calamity.

In due course I had the measles and cut my teeth and sustained all the other adventures incident to babyhood. It must have been no sinecure to bring me up. Whenever my mother took me off to bed I used to screech so furiously that half the town would assemble in front of our house in the belief I was being murdered...

Nine o'clock! Where's my cold cream, grease paint, wig, clarinet and fiddle? Another half-hour and I must show the world

that it simply cannot do without Grock. It
is becoming increasingly difficult for me to
prove this point. My critics and managers
continue to make it so. How to live up to
all their splutter of superlatives? I find it
takes it out of me more and more, this in-
cessant stress and strain to surpass the
bounds Nature allotted me.

To-day I bought a book from a bookstall
—one of the greatest literary successes of all
time, so the bookseller informed me. *The
Life and Opinions of Tristram Shandy*. I
couldn't put it down, but read and read, and
kept turning over the pages. A book to read
and a book to talk of, this colossal kaleido-
scope of many colours, this gallimaufry of
dates and happenings jostled all together
and emptied out on to the table, to be re-
assembled either as their own stark selves,
or veneered with the author's comments and
personal predilections. That's right down
my street ... that's the writer for me!

But when Tristram Shandy says that of all
worlds ever created this world is the most
vile, then I, Grock would like to say: "It
is better than this trade of yours! Oh, yes,
my dear sir, for this vilest of worlds has

granted to us, its inhabitants, not only a tolerable existence but the power to extract mirth for millions out of nothing and less than nothing—a wig, a stick of grease paint, a child's fiddle, a chair without a seat. I rather think, Mr. Shandy, that the fault lies not so much within your world as within yourself."

And this power to make something out of nothing is given to all of us. All we need is the will to do it. To that eternal naïve question reporters are for ever shouting at me: "Why did you become a clown?" I have only one reply. "Because I wanted to."

In the town of my childhood's days lived a certain eminent and distinguished worthy, Fritz Bloesch, our local Crœsus. Fritz Bloesch had to his credit three daughters, pretty girls all, the best garden in the town, the best horses, the best dogs, real prize-winning beauties, as you could tell by the way they bayed. Fritz Bloesch went about in his old age always dressed in the smartest of suits with a flower in his buttonhole, and when he drove through the streets in his wagonette, sitting on the box-seat, he would look like happiness personified. Not that he

17

was in the least stuck-up. Far from it; he was always simple, affable and charming. He liked to be taken notice of and would return all salutations smilingly with a wave of his whip. On the 6th of December, when St. Nicholas day came round, all the children of Bienne would be in a frenzy of excitement, for Fritz Bloesch would never fail to put in an appearance, fatherly and beaming, at the Gingerbread Fair held near the old Town Hall, where he would distribute cakes and goodies with handshakes galore. I remember shaking him by the hand once, and a good, warm, stout hand it was.

One day my mother said to me: "D'you suppose you'll ever be able to earn a decent living by tight-roping and pulling faces?"

"Oh, yes," I answered her. "I'll be as rich one day as Fritz Bloesch."

I have no notion of the precise sum that went to make up the deposit account of Fritz Bloesch at the bank, but I do know this: that to-day the money I earn at least enables me to indulge in the whimsies and fancies that served to delight Fritz Bloesch in his day.

3

THE COW-HERD DRESSED-UP

To-DAY was pay-day. What I think I say.
They all think as I do, but very few
say it. Come now, own up, all of you,
you are like sleuth-hounds on the track of
filthy lucre!

I'm not indifferent to money. Not on your
life! Money is power. This bundle of notes
I hold in my hand positively *does* emit radio-
active rays.

I can feel my very muscles hardening and
the swelling of my breast. For I am behold-
ing the rock of defence from which I can defy
the world—or make it, rather, more cordial
and friendly towards me.

For the world is so full of discontent that
one of these days it will collapse altogether,
being unable to carry on any more. In my
mind's eye I can already see America crash-
ing on one hand and England on the
other, weltering in the universal slime, the
boot of Italy cracking along a line described

by Genoa, Milan and Venice, France and Germany rotting from the earth's axis and spinning after them. Even Switzerland, the stoical, has had enough of it. Basle, Geneva, Zürich, join in the universal slither. All but one little piece of Switzerland joins in. That little piece stands steadfast now and for ever and a day. The world must have *one* solid fragment as a rock-bottom base. The name of that fragment is Berne.

My faith in Berne and the Bernerland will endure when I have ceased to believe in everything else. Those little cities of the Bernerland, Burgdorf, Langenthal, Langnau, Thun, Frutigen, and the ancient town of Berne itself will sit tight throughout the chaos of the last Judgment Day. They are used to it. Worlds may crash around them to their hearts' content, and should one chicken-hearted citizen among their number so much as whisper it were perhaps as well to test the stability of their own foundations, a chorus of gruff, bass voices will reply: "Mir wei de oppe luege" . . . "there's time yet, to see about that" . . .

I am constantly told I am like a "cowherd, dressed-up" on the stage. Well, that's one up to me, then. For I hail from the Bernese Oberland, and am my father' son from Reichenbach, near Frutigen. Only as clown do I go by the name of Grock. As citizen and ratepayer my name is Wettach.

The Wettachs have dwelt in Reichenbach for generations. The old village lies in the "Kiental" at the beginning of one of the largest valleys of the Bernese Alps. Way back of the Kiental the mountains raise their heads to heaven, so dazzling white you cannot look at them for more than two minutes together, with their glaciers and their snow-fields and the great, dazzling "Bluemlisalp." For generations past the Wettachs have been cow-herds from father to son.

A Bernese peasant is the solidest object ever rooted in this earth. He is in it up to the chest. His arms and head are still left free for him to wave, but the rest of him is encased in the good earth. That's the stock I come from.

In the Municipal Offices of Reichenbach a great book is kept, huge as a flake of rock from the "Bluemlisalp." It contains the ancient record of all the valley population, and the Wettachs are in it too from generation to generation. It gives me a sense of pride, this feeling of *growing* out of the place where I was born, instead of just happening by chance. My great-grandfather has gone down to posterity in no less than two pages of that book. He was an innkeeper by trade, in Frutigen, and though he could not rival our great Bernese man of war, Adrian von Bubenberg, the doughty opponent of Charles the Fifth, who had three hundred and fifty children to his credit, at least my great-grandfather could record twenty. Last summer, when I was in Reichenbach looking at this record, I surreptitiously pulled out my fountain pen, and in an unguarded moment added "Grock" to the name of Adrien Wettach. A clown now stood enrolled with all these hundreds of cow-herds and peasants. Truly the ways of our Creator are passing strange at times!

From Oslo to Buenos Aires I am acclaimed as the the most versatile human product of our age. None the less, I am a proper Bernese, and smack of my origin, inasmuch as Wettach, of Reichenbach, near Frutigen, has become Grock, the Clown of All the World,

EVEN AS AN INFANT I SHOWED EVERY SIGN
OF PROMISE

AGED 6 AT COL DE ROCHES

who can slip, on demand, through the eye of a needle. It is only your Swiss, and above all your Bernese-born, who can turn himself into your perfect acrobat, tight-rope dancer and clown. For we Swiss are essentially a serious and law-abiding folk. *Les extrêmes se touchent!*

Switzerland is the calmest country on this earth. But a country full of calmness will always contain plenty of unrest. The calmness of the Swiss is an elemental calm, and so is its unrest. One has only to think of the fifteenth century. The Burgundy wars were past then, the great battles of Grandson, Murten and Nancy had all been fought; Charles the Bold, who tried to reduce Berne to ashes, had had his head clubbed into a pulp. One of us Wettachs, or so they say, fought at Nancy; it might even have been this ancestor of mine who cracked the mighty Charles's skull.

After which Switzerland, for nearly a quarter of a century, knew no more war. Such a state of somnolence was not to be endured for long. One fine Sunday all the fighting spirits assembled in Lucerne, sporting a banner with a boar worked on it. Five hundred strong, they marched westwards towards the Lake of Geneva, hewing and smiting all before them on their way. They couldn't help themselves. They *must* have their war. The procession marched into Berne two thousand strong, and by the time it got to the Lake of Geneva numbered four thousand.

But soon Switzerland settled down once again to peace and quiet. Her unruly members now fared forth to fight under alien banners and foreign captains. All one to them who the foe was, provided they could lay about them; in the mighty battle of Novara, Swiss fought against Swiss, each killing the other dead. Swiss defended the Tuileries against the Revolution, and were mowed down to a man. Ten thousand Swiss allowed themselves to be killed in the service of Napoleon. What of the present day? What shall the turbulent Swiss do now that his country has congealed hard and compact as an uncutable cheese that a man must needs smash with a hammer?

My father had this typical Swiss restlessness in his blood. The way he dragged us about from pillar to post! We were never in one place for more than two years together. He came into this world a hundred years too late. Napoleon the Great—*he* would have been the man for him!

We soon left Neuveville for Landeron that lies somewhat further westward between the two lakes, the Lake of Bienne on one side, serene and mild, and on the other the Lake of Neuchâtel, huge and sombre, while southwards, of an evening, glowed the Alps. The gloomy and antiquated little city of Landeron had Roman remains and towers. Its houses were built upon wine-cellars, and you had only to shut a door to set the echoes thundering down the steep stone stairs that led into the vaults. The whole of Landeron reeked of wine.

I was four when we went to Landeron but I remember very little about it. I have dim recollections still of the forest at Jolimont, I can see the vines growing on the Jura slopes and hear the rustle of reeds by the lake side. I remember I had a playmate three years older than I was, called Wiedmer, who smelt always of butter and cheese. At vintage time in the autumn we would steal among the vines, and eat our bellyful of grapes till we could eat no more. After which I would pierce a hole in my straw hat, fill it with grapes and squash them all together till the juice ran over me. I would be a mass of grape juice from head to foot when I reached home, and dire was the penalty my father would exact for the crime.

One February day we couple of imps crept down through the reeds to the lake for a bathe! I was shaking like Jack Frost when my mother came to look for me and fetch me home. For many days afterwards I lay seriously ill, but my fever and high temperature were all magicked away finally by egg whipped up with sugar.

My most excellent Mother! Egg whipped up with sugar was her universal panacea. Ever since I can remember I have loved a "scrap." I have tussled with all my colleagues, clowns and accomplices, and the dressing-rooms of circuses and music-halls have resounded the world over to the slaps I have given and received. Even in the Landeron days I felt the need for a scrap, and each day I would come home with my full share of bruises and cuts. But I had only to cross the threshold, howling, for my mother to

open the kitchen cupboard, take out an
egg, whip it up and sugar it with the
words:

"Here's your egg, Adrien ... drink it up
quick ... and it will all be all right ..."

4

ONION MUSIC AND MY FIRST CIRCUS

WE Wettachers like to chop and change and simply don't know what it is to rust. There wasn't enough *tang* in the air of dark and dismal Landeron to suit our lungs. Our time there came to an end and for the next stage of our life's journey my father chose Le Locle, that big village of a hundred watch factories that lies in the Neuchâtel Jura. We children shrieked with delight at the thought of change and another move. The world about us had been standing still for so long, but now, once again, it was beginning to open its eyes and whirl around.

Packing up began. All day long the old house would be filled with the sound of hammering, while boxes and luggage cluttered up the rooms and passages. To my special care were entrusted the onion ropes that hung from the ceiling between the beams in great golden clusters. I had to undo them

from their strings and pack them neatly
away into boxes.

What are onions and onion ropes, anyway? What are they *for?* From my point of
view, for something quite other than the purpose to which cold common sense has allotted them since the time of Abraham. Ever
since I can remember, all kinds of inanimate
objects have had a way of looking at me reproachfully and whispering to me in unguarded moments: "We've been waiting for
you... at last you've come ... take us now,
and turn us into something different . . .
we've been so *bored*, waiting ..." I believe
the secret of success lies in looking at the
world like that—in seeing it every day of
one's life as though for the very first time.
The rest comes automatically. To use onions
for nothing but frying and making into sauce
... how humdrum . . . how unimaginative!
Think of all the other things onions could
do. One of them is to make the most marvellous music, all their own.

I've tried it and I know. I've got the most
tremendous pleasure out of onion music. In
all Swiss cottages, the "privy" is built into a
corner at the back, and connected with the

pit below by a long and hollow wooden shaft made of four boards. One morning I had an inspiration. Nobody being at home, I unhooked an onion-rope from its peg and taking it with me raised up the familiar seat, and let the golden balls drop into the depth below, so that they knocked and jostled against the wooden planks in their passage.

Rhythm and sound have always, from my earliest childhood, excited me beyond measure, and now that I was actually, *ex officio*, so to say, in possession of no less than a hundred strings of onions, I now fairly succumbed to temptation and resolved to set a whole orchestra in action. So once again I removed the seat and dispatched one string of onions after another down the wooden shaft. *"Gulugulugulu patsch,"* they said, *"gulugulugulugulu bumm patsch"* . . . just like a Hottentot dance . . . *"gulubumm"* . . . over and over again, nine and ninety times. Imagine my enchantment! I was just starting off the hundredth string on its appointed task when my grandmother descended upon me like a whirlwind, though not in time to stop me from sending the last golden ball rolling.

"Isn't it fun, granny . . . isn't it awful fun?" . . .

Her only reply was to seize me by the scruff of my neck and lay me across her knee. I don't think I have ever had the seat of my breeches pulled so tight, before or since. But I bore it all with indifference, thinking of how my mother would come to me with her unfailing remedy, egg beaten up with sugar. Not till she came up to me with my braces instead of the healing draught did I give myself up to the pain of my tingling behind.

The great day came for us to leave the vineyard country and go up into the mountains. It was the middle of the vintage season, and the air was full of the smell of crushed grapes. Just to snuff it you could almost think you were drinking them. The vats were groaning, the grape-gatherers singing and dancing, while between the rows of vines shimmered the Lake of Neuchâtel, with the mighty Bernese Alps behind it. A great day, indeed.

Le Locle itself was not nearly so exciting. My recollection of the place is hazy, but I vividly remember the day that ended our sojourn there, and all the days that came after it. We moved up to the Col des Roches, by the French frontier. There we found forest after forest, and blue gentian blooming and pasture land with cows and horses. The people were friendly towards us and the Café National, that my father had taken over, did a thriving trade.

One morning the whole village was suffused with excitement, especially we children who broke loose from school in the middle of a class, and swarmed into the village square, whence the schoolmaster had to come and collect us, driving us back, stick in hand. What had happened? A travelling circus had arrived. With eyes popping out of our heads we surrounded the miserable pair of circus wagons with their tiny curtained windows behind which everything was as quiet as quiet could be, for the inhabitants were fast asleep, their skinny horses peacefully cropping the grass at their feet, the while.

During the entire afternoon the young fry of the village stood glued to the spot witnessing the exciting procedure of the tent pegs being driven into the ground and the canvas being fixed to the great pole. Imagine our ecstasy when night fell and upon the platform erected in front of the tent the artists paraded in the glare of the naptha lamps, inciting the public to enter by their jokes and their antics. The troupe consisted mainly of seven children in rose-red tights, with a big, jovial man at their head, with a white-chalked face and scarlet nose and mouth. For the first time in my life I beheld a CLOWN, and for the first time also felt something stir within me that was not just mere childhood excitement. That something said to me: I WILL. I *will* become what that man is there upon the platform.

And now the show began to the sound of trumpet and drum. I, as one unworthy of the Promised Land, must perforce stay outside. But I soon discovered a hole in the canvas tent. Through it I beheld the entire circus, and stood there rapt in a dream of colour and dance. Indeed, had my mother not come out to fetch me home I think I should be standing there still, my feet rooted in the ground, lost in ecstasy.

School next morning was attended by a terrible Inquisition, with all its tears and punishments. I returned home in the most *piano* frame of mind, to find a broad-shouldered, amiable-looking man with big moustachios standing at the bar. I knew him at once as the comedian of the previous evening, and my father introduced me to him as his seven-year-old son. I was proud as Punch, and prouder still to find the familiar way my father had with this clown, slapping him on the shoulder and calling him " old boy " with no uncertain voice.

This clown, named Wetzel, was actually the director of the circus, and an old friend of my father's. Wetzel was the brother-in-law of Ricono, the proprietor of that very circus from whence my grandmother had extracted my father at the age of seventeen, with the assistance of the police, during a rehearsal. Later on, Wetzel became a stout friend to me, and his sound advice has often stood me in good stead.

Unfortunately the circus was not allowed to stay its full time, owing to the schoolmaster complaining to the local authorities that it was detrimental to youthful morals. So good fellow Wetzel was off and away, with his children, two carts and four horses, attended by all the youthful inhabitants of Col des Roches, who walked by their side till the forest began. There we left them, and as we turned on our homeward way it seemed to me as though the valley betwixt the wooded hills was still flooded with a streak of rainbow light.

Soon after this I drove a stake into the ground behind our house to which I fastened a piece of canvas I had begged from the greengrocer on my mother's behalf. I instituted a circus, to which I invited the whole village, myself playing the double rôle of acrobat and clown, for which purpose I had purloined chalk and red ink from the schoolhouse. The performance was a huge success and repeated more than once. It was about this time that I received my first piano lessons from my father on a piano that the inn contained. But our Col des Roches period had by now come to an end, and my father had decided to move on to Replatte, a village below Le Locle. Once again we started out in high-piled carts, care-free and merry as ever when we fared forth into the great unknown. Amongst our household goods the piano took a prominent place, and I sat on a beer barrel in front of it, embracing the keys with a masterly touch, till the welkin

35

rang to the sound of the old Bernese march and "Sempacherlied."

"Lasst hören aus alter Zeit von kühner Ahnen Heldenstreit. . ."

But now things were about to change and bad days begin. We had never had to pinch so much before. They put me out to service with a peasant named Bachmann. I had to herd his cows and milk them, clean out their byre, cut the hay, plant the potatoes and chop the wood. For all this I got a litre of milk every day plus forty centimes, and a pair of wooden sabots. I was as pleased as Punch to be able to help in the upkeep of the home, for even in those days I could never feel things were going well with me if they were not going well with my nearest and dearest. When I analyse myself and ask: "What is your most deep-rooted impulse, where are you most sensitive and easily wounded?" the answer always is: "My *family sense . . ."*

Two whole years of Replatte! The thought of it is like a great grey cavern. Finally my father plumped for the town that beyond all doubt was created for us and ours. Dear Bienne! We were surely secret citizens of yours long before we knew you, before we had so much as sniffed a breath of your air into our lungs. We belong, part and parcel, to Bienne on the Lake, and thither did we peregrinate over the mountains to the city in the valley that is dearer to my heart than all other towns in the world.

5

A GOOD THICK SKIN

My Berlin season is coming to an end, and to-morrow I must move on to Cologne. Once again I must pack up my make-up box, together with my press notices. The latter is a mighty tome full of superlatives, bristling with Bravos and Bravissimos and the plaudits of the Press of Münich, Frankfort, Essen, Düsseldorf, Marseilles, Lyons, Budapest, Milan and Brussels; all these pages here are Paris, then comes Berlin, that simply doesn't know how to crack me up sufficiently. "The terrific Grock ... Grock the priceless, the inimitable, the irresistible, the incomparable, the devastating ... Grock the man of genius ... Grock the Divine" ... *Divine?* Well— all I can say is, there the word stands! And I should be a liar, were I to tell you I find this blare of trumpets unpleasing to my ear. I like to see proof positive of the fact that I *click*. I've no desire to hold a monologue with myself in the desert of Sahara.

MY DÉBUT IN THE HOUSE OF PARADISE

Paul Rüedi   ST. JMIER

THE BOY'S A PRODIGY!

Nine months of the year I spend my life as
Silly Billy. Surely I have all the more need
to ask to be taken seriously while on holiday.
Nine months of the year I pass amid the
glare of the footlights and the stale atmosphere of a theatrical dressing-room. The remaining three months I revel in the opposite
extreme—surrounded by the good smell of
earth and reek of dung. The scent of flowers
too—that's a weak spot of mine. My house
on the Riviera is smothered in flowers. I
have deliberately seen to it that this is so, to
counteract the fumes of the great Italian oil
factory close by. And there are three tip-top
workrooms in my house, moreover—one for
carpentering, one for locksmithery, and one
for watch-making. Am I not a watch-maker's
son?

I am passionately interested in clocks and
their insides. I collect clocks and watches.
I am quite capable of getting up in the middle
of the night, being unable to sleep through
the irregular strike or ticking of some clock
on the wall. Up I get and bear the invalid off
to my workroom, where I dissect it down to
its minutest part, and never dream of returning to bed till my patient is restored safe

and sound to its wall.

There goes the warning-bell! Time to go up on the stage now. How often have I done this before? Well, according to my latest reckoning, I should say about ten thousand times! But my ten thousandth appearance before the footlights finds me just as nervy as the day I made my first bow, thirty-seven years ago.

No sooner do I get upon the stage than all my self-protective armour peels away from me and I am a recording instrument as sensitive as a mimosa plant. There is nothing I cannot feel and nothing I do not react to. Last night's audience, for instance! Never have I found it more heavy-going work. What's the use of all my printed encomiums when I am fully aware of not having struck one single spark throughout one entire turn? As a general rule there the hydra-headed monster sits, a prey to convulsive laughter, waving its thousand arms at me like a gigantic polypus, and I ensconce myself in their midst in a state of the utmost complacency. But yesterday there it sat, with tentacles all tight and drawn-in, a veritable blank wall of human flesh. There I was anticking in

front of it, with precisely the same gam-
bols and jests as on every other evening, and
yet—not a sound. Somehow or another it
seemed impossible to establish any kind of
contact, or hardly any.

You all know that *deadly* feeling in the air
when there is thunder about that cannot
burst forth and release itself in lightning, but
still stays perforce within its prison of cloud.
That is what happened to me last night. No
wonder I didn't sleep a wink. It's a dreadful
thing to be charged up like a battery, with no
outlet but one's self.

But a real downright frost . . . a complete
and absolute *flop*—have I ever had one?
Wait while I tell you. Oh, there's that bell
again! All the same I will tell you, in as few
words as possible, before I have to go on,
about the greatest fiasco in all my career. It
happened in Berlin in 1911. Dear old Antonet was my fellow unfortunate. The
Winter Garden had sent for us to come from
Scheveningen, where we had been with the
Schumann Circus. We were being billed
everywhere as "ANTONET AND GROCK,
THE WORLD'S GREATEST CLOWNS,"
and we certainly had had four consecutive

weeks' terrific success at Scheveningen. So famous and talked-of had we become that a great German music-hall combine was offering to engage us for a period of fourteen weeks at a salary of four thousand marks a month. That in itself meant the approbation of no less than twenty-two managers.

To get back to the Winter Garden! The two and twenty managers sat before us in a row in the stalls on our first night. In due course we made our entrance in the approved circus fashion, a couple of conquering heroes in brand new frock coats: Kubelik and Rubinstein. Antonet was bedizened with orders and be-gewgawed as any perambulating merry-go-round, but nothing could have surpassed the air of superiority with which he turned to me and said:—

"Introduce me, please, Rubinstein, to these ladies and gentlemen."

"Ladies and Gentlemen, I have the honour to present to you Professor Kubelik, the greatest violinist that ever has been or ever will be. Professor Kubelik, as you see, has already had medals bestowed upon him from all quarters of the world—three French gold medals, eight silver and ten Certificates of

Merit; seven gold English medals, twelve silver and thirteen Certificates of Merit; from Russia seventeen gold medals, twenty-eight silver and forty-three Diplomas of Merit, while from the land of Spaghetti and Tomatoes he has already acquired no less than twenty-five gold medals, thirty-nine silver and seventy-two Diplomas of Merit . . ."

We were accustomed to just this bare enumeration throwing our circus audience into convulsions of merriment. But our Berlin public never moved an eyelash. Whereupon Kubelik takes up his position with an air of supreme disdain and I, as his accompanist, sit down to the piano.

"What are you looking for, Rubinstein?"

"The tuning crank, Herr Geheimrat. The keys want tuning up."

"Nonsense. Crank yourself! It's your two hands you want to use—not a crank! Come now, begin . . ."

Again I sit down and frantically attack the keyboard, as though I would pound the notes before me to a jelly But not a sound results except for the dull knocking of the felted hammers and the wheezing of the notes. I

43

get down from my stool.

"The brute's sick, Your Excellency!"

I fumble about with the keyboard, grope among the pedals, open the sounding-board. A pistol shot resounds from the wings.

"There! That's a string broke ... bass has gone futt. Why ... what ... this is a *piano*, not a *wardrobe!*" On which I extract from the piano's entrails an enormous length of wire, and a pair of crimson corsets of monstrous dimensions. On which the audience should simply be holding its sides, every member of it! But no. Not a hand. They just sat there, staring, in stony silence and disapproval. A living iceberg.

Once we get into the wings for our quick change we look volumes at each other. My heart is in my boots, or rather it has slithered out into the orchestra and is hiding in the big drum. We've missed fire . . . altogether missed fire ... We finish the turn in the most mechanical and dismal fashion, and once the merciful curtain has come down at last I am quite resolved to give up the mummer's profession for ever and a day. We creep back to our dressing-room, where we bolt the door, and sitting on our baskets stare straight before us into space. Being quite unable to contain myself for any length of time, I burst out crying, and Antonet joins in, a key higher. It would melt a heart of stone to have seen Antonet and Grock, "the world's greatest clowns," crying their eyes out that August night of 1911 in their dressing-room in the Winter Gardens, Berlin. We must have looked a pretty couple of guys, our painted faces smeared all over with tears. If only our audience could have seen us like that!

A sharp rap on the door brought us down to earth. We recognised the voice of Marinelli, our agent. I opened the door. Marinelli exploded when he caught sight of my face, like a great, wet, swollen pear. But he soon became grave again:

"Boys ... boys ... what on earth have you been thinking of? A music-hall isn't a *circus!* You're too broad ... altogether too broad. Tone it down and suit your stuff to variety . . ."

He had hit the nail on the head. It's one thing to have your audience all round you, and another in front of you. Your turn in the circus ring must be bold and exaggerated, even over-exaggerated, but a music-hall turn must be altogether on a smaller scale, much more sharply defined. So we repeated our circus turn in terms of variety. But in vain, all of it. We had repeated failures on the second, third and fourth evenings, and on the fifth, before our turn began, we found all our twenty-two contracts displayed for our inspection. Cancelled, every one of them!

It was touch and go now with a vengeance. Both our careers were at stake. From eleven o'clock that night till seven the next morning we were closeted together in our hotel room, evolving a new turn, something that should be essentially "of the halls," none of your "ad lib" business, everything cut and dried. Antonet was to play an *aria* on his violin from *Traviata,* myself accompanying him on the concertina, after which I should bring my comic "cricket fiddle" out of its case and let it chirrup. We would end up with a regular Bernese *jodel* and a dance. We had got it all ready by nine.

That evening beheld us triumphant! And our triumph lasted, too, for four whole weeks one after another, during which those managers who had given us the go-by turned up again to a man. Butter wouldn't melt in their mouths, now!

"Those old contracts? I should think not, indeed! We're asking a thousand marks a month more now—just to learn you!"

I knew the rascals *wanted* us, good and proper.

"But Grock, my dear old boy . . ."

"None of that now. Fair words butter no parsnips. Yes or no?"

I stood by the door, latch in hand. A significant gesture, and it worked. The thousand marks were agreed to on the nail. My manager was a witness of the proceedings.

"Well, Grock, you're a big clown all right . . . but as a business man you're even bigger . . ."

That warmed me to the cockles of my heart, for it gave me visions of myself as a really first-rate man of affairs.

I relate this little episode for the benefit of my colleagues in Variety and Circus. Never be modest! Ask terms that make your partner simply sweat with horror! The world sets a high value on the man who knows how to value himself. My recipe is good, believe me. To have the goods to offer is an excellent thing in itself, but at rock-bottom it's an artist's salary that makes his reputation. I've been there, and I know. An artist is worth what he makes himself worth. Not elevating, perhaps—but true!

A man whose life it is to turn somersaults and twist himself into knots, eat fire and ice and glass, to say nothing of the circus dust that must needs fill his lungs, can't last like ordinary men. 'Tisn't everyone who's composed of barbed wire, as I am. He must have as much recoil in him as a Parabellum pistol.

And above all things he must have a good, thick skin! He must be armour-plated as an armadillo. It's the only way to carry on. Never have I had more need of armour-plate than in this incredible city of Berlin, where Fate has played so many crazy pranks with me. It saw me, many years ago, in my direst poverty. While to-day it sees me as a distinguished celebrity, rocked on the frothy, perilous waves of worldly success!

I have taken a long farewell of the city, this very day as ever is. I actually retraced the steps that, many years ago, I trod so painfully on foot. There was the corner where I

used to stand by the Leipziger-Friedrich-
strasse. But I was not standing now. In
those days I had just ten pfennigs in my
pocket and was revolving the important question whether to blue them on a glass of beer
at Aschinger's or go for a ride in an omnibus
to the Oranienburgertor. Whereas to-day I
sit at the wheel of my 150 PS Isotta Fraschini waiting for the green light to start with
the traffic.

Curtain up, did you say? All right, I'm
a-coming . . . I'm a-coming . . .

6

THE ARTISTE AS IDEAL CITIZEN

WELCOME to Cologne! I like Cologne. At my first appearance last night the house was sold out, and I had no less than twelve calls. The Press has been unanimous in my praises and the advance booking indicates another packed audience for to-night.

It is I who fill the hall on this occasion from floor to ceiling, but the music-halls are doing well, too, in my absence. The cult of the music-hall is in tune with the modern spirit that likes this perpetual catch-ball we artistes play with the actual happenings of the age we live in.

But how little you know of us really, you spectators. There we stand before you on the stage or in the ring, beglamoured with all the world's romance and mirth. The music-hall artiste knows nothing of Time, Space or Age. He has subdued these three ghostly spectres for all to behold. I have known men of sixty-five years turning somersaults like boys of twenty, so strung-up would they be, once called upon to face the footlights. Nothing is impossible to your true artiste. This tremendous discipline of the will to which he subjected himself as a youngster, serves him in good stead now the years come thick upon him, so that he can still move mountains. We artistes view life from a point that is simplicity itself. It is the *will* that moves us, nothing less and nothing more. It is both our benefactor and our torment.

An actor of the "legitimate stage" can go sick, and failing to appear at the last moment his place can be taken by his understudy. Not so with artistes of our kidney. We carry our bag of tricks within ourselves; no other person upon earth can read the riddle of our secret. Understudies are out of the question. Only death can excuse him from appearing. I know what I'm talking about, or at least I ought to. I've experienced it often enough, and never more painfully than in that year of horror 1911, when I was within an ace of having hand and arm amputated through blood-poisoning. The time had even been fixed for the operation and a room engaged for me in the hospital, but in spite of it all I set my teeth and won through. It was in the Berlin Winter Garden that I had to cut all my maddest capers to disguise the most appalling pain. I was beside myself with agony and the public beside itself with merriment; so soon as my turn was ended the stream of blood I had managed up till now to repress got the better of me and spurted through the bandage. I staggered back into my dressing-room and screamed like a stuck pig.

Well—what of it, anyway? If I'd a hundred lives at my disposal I'd never want to be anything but a music-hall artiste. There's something about my profession that's irresistible, or so I think—this mastering by will-power, this transforming the little, everyday annoyances, not only overcoming, but actually *transforming* them into some strange and terrific.

We slither down from our heights after the show, like a climber down the slopes of Chimborazo, and having dwindled again to mortal proportions have one wish and only one; to shuffle into our carpet-slippers, light our pipe, sit behind the stove and be nothing but citizens, ordinary, humdrum citizens, the more humdrum the better. All the members of our audience who have sat agape and hand-clapping, have stolen away from their fire-sides and the constraints of domesticity, try-ing to forget the narrowness of their lives in our "comic cuts"; when the show is over, and not till then, they will creep back home to the old frowsty nest. If they only knew how those anticking in front of them envied them this same nest!

Your theatre-artiste is the ideal citizen. The greater part of his day is spent in hectic, exacting conditions, facing danger. Some sort of compensation for this he must have, and so he fills the rest of his time with crea-ture comfort and humdrumness.

We theatre folk are no gipsies. We have a strong sense of convention. I doubt whether the most solid bourgeois families can count stricter principles and habits or more respect-able marriages to their credit than we can. You, parents, don't you worry if your child-ren want to adopt our profession. Let them get on with it! It's not we who manufacture bombs of dynamite, it's not we that are the Bolshies! Our calling is grounded on a basis of good solid respectability, and your theatre artiste, more than any other human wight, compelled to lead a life that's orderly.

My most whimsical flights in no way conflict with my argument that I am domestic to the very marrow. Any dressing-room occupied by me is clean as a new pin. The lid fits tight on to my powder-box, my dressing-table is guiltless of any smear or stain from grease or paint. My pots of "make-up" stand in a sedate row, in the order they are used. My mirror shines, flawless. My coat is smoothed faultlessly over the chair-back, with my trousers folded neatly upon it. Below are placed my shoes in the correct position, all to a hair's breadth. My socks . . . no, they are not lying crumpled up into a ball . . . they are carefully displayed across the shoes. World-fame or no, I continue to mend them myself.

I keep my things like anything. There are men, I know, whose things look like nothing on earth after they have had them a few days only. They seem to have a special power to wear out garments. I have no gifts in this direction. The longer I keep my things the better they seem to be and I am proud of the fact.

Music-hall dressing-rooms, except in Eng-

"HANDY LAD"

PHOTO TAKEN FOR ADELAIDE, IN 1905

land and America, are not what they should be. Every English music-hall that pays decent terms, has its dressing-room with water laid on. The London Coliseum, the best and most famous music-hall in the world, provides its dressing-rooms with shower baths and every kind of hygienic comfort. But on the Continent we theatre folk are miserably provided for. All the money is spent on the audience. For them the theatre proprietors simply cannot do enough. They must have plenty of light, plenty of space, plenty of silk and satin upholstery. Anything is good enough for the artiste. In the big music-halls in both Paris and Lyons, the dressing-rooms are directly underneath the stage. Masses of dust and dirt are danced down upon our heads during each performance. Such things should not be. We are forced to swallow quite enough dust and powder as it is, in our profession.

Give me, rather than that, the four poles and bit of canvas of the travelling circus! Your basket is then your make-up table, with a guttering candle perched upon it as you hold a fragment of glass in your hand for mirror. Many a time have I painted and pow-

dered myself so, amid the rain, the snow and
the wind. Lucky for me that I had a hide as
thick as a huntsman's. The piece of sail-
cloth gets bellied out by the wind, a sharp
gust blows out the stump of candle, and all is
wrapped in darkness. That is the moment
the Ring Master usually chooses to stick his
head through an opening of the tent and roar
"Your turn, Wettach, now!" I grope around
me in the gloom for my wooden sabots, slip
my feet into them, cursing, and, with the rain
driving me full in the face, paddle along
through puddles and dung, till I arrive, with
a bound, in the ring.

I shall never forget a certain dressing-
room in Hungary, many years ago. In the
dog-days of a particularly hot summer I was
trapesing from village to village as acrobat
and clown with a travelling circus. I used to
instal myself underneath the wagon where
we kept our luggage, and there I would sleep,
and get myself ready for our next performance. But when we trudged on our way
through the interminable countryside past
cabbage fields and fields of maize, and provender was in sight, I would slip from my
hiding place out into the fields, and return

with great armfuls—as full as I could make them. I became both cook and commissariat for the whole troupe. My grateful colleagues were never tired of praising my culinary triumphs as day after day, for a period of many weeks, I continued to transform my stolen provender into meals for their support.

Never have I slept sounder than in this little hanging contraption under the wagon where we stowed our "props" away. It used to rock to and fro, and I may be said virtually to have rocked myself half round Hungary! An ideal method of locomotion! But one night I had a rude awakening, and had perforce to cling on with both hands to prevent myself being hurled into space. In my half-awakened state, my first impression was that the Day of Judgment had arrived. Lurid flames of fire were streaming up into the sky, while the thunder all around must surely mean the imminent destruction of every town and mountain. I could hear, borne away upon the wind, the cries of my colleagues. At the risk of my life I crept out of my crazy resting place, and was just in time to help fasten up the horses, all of them on the verge of running amok.

7

THE "VARIABLE STAR" CITY

I HAVE never had a great deal of truck with books. I hadn't time, when I was young; I was too busy, living. And nowadays I have grown somewhat mistrustful of them; I have probably got to know too many book producers of late years. I purchased an old tome this summer from one of the booksellers' stalls in Paris on the Quai de la Cité. My attention was attracted by an engraving on the first page: my own ugly phiz, looking at me! Underneath it was written the name Marius. I turned over the leaves and proceeded to read the chapter that dealt with Marius the Roman. There was a fellow for you! He didn't let the grass grow under his feet—not he! The book was written by a Grecian of the Roman age, called Plutarch. Can we to-day, I wonder, improve upon the maxims that Plutarch stood for in his lifetime?

I still most vividly remember some reading

I did many years ago in Hungary in the country house of Count Bethlen. During all that sultry summer, full of thunder, I would ride my horse, Lila, around the countryside all day, and at night lie in my room poring over the dramas of Corneille and Racine, bound in one volume. Somehow I think I caught the noble spirit and mighty simplicity of these great works.

Hungary! My recollections of Hungary still warm the cockles of my heart. But first I must tell how I got there. That's harking back a great way, back to my youth where I last left off. I left off in Bienne, that town "that surely was created for us and ours."

Bienne is positively unique among all the towns of Europe. Although it must be at least a hundred times smaller than Berlin, the mighty, it is none the less a little world within itself. Never have I seen so much bustle and activity within a little space. The inhabitants of Bienne are three-fifths of them German Swiss and the remaining two-fifths French Swiss. Both German and French lessons are given in the schools. The Parliamentary debates are held in both languages, and in the principal church a sermon is

preached every Sunday at nine in German
and in French at eleven. The Fire Brigade
puts out your fire for you both in German and
French. Of course everyone living in Bienne
can speak either language. The Germans
speak French much like a bear dancing on a
tight-rope, while the French emit the German
gutturals like sugar-plums between their
teeth. Both nations are the best of friends,
and a blend of the two is a rare and most
excellent product.

Strictly speaking, the natives of Bienne are
Swiss, and yet they are Swiss with a difference. They are the best athletes and the best
makers of brass musical instruments in all
Switzerland, and yet they are known to be
the least stable, temperamentally, of all our
population. A Swiss has only got to be known
to hail from Bienne and he is immediately regarded dubiously and with suspicion.

Most of the Swiss bankrupts come from
Bienne. Bienne is the inevitable and natural
focus of all booths and places of tomfoolery.
The Hiplehs, the Weiffenbachs, the Wallendas, the Leilichs, for generations on end have
been showing there their jugglers, wax figures
and misbegotten monsters that serve them for

a living at the yearly fairs held betwixt Nancy and Innsbruck. They love Bienne. It is their spiritual home. All the ne'er-do-wells between the Jura and the Alps take refuge within its gates, all rogues and wastrels and those that live from hand to mouth. It was born, surely, beneath a "variable star." And in this city it was that the Wettachs came to dwell. Optimistic as ever, and full of our usual trust in God, we began this new stage of our existence.

My father had bought himself another inn at Bienne—the "House of Paradise." It certainly was a house of Paradise for us children. The big garden was a veritable grove of chestnut trees, and an enormous drive of these huge trees, some of which must have been two hundred years old, led right away to the city gates. The Jura mountains rose sheer above our house, and we had only to scramble a certain distance up the rocky slopes to find ourselves in the heart of the mountain forest, with its wild raspberries and strawberries and grotesque boulders borne down by the Alpine glaciers since time immemorial.

But if you went the other way down

through the meadows and crossed the mole
you would reach the pasture land by the lake,
my sweet, beloved Lake of Bienne. On one
shore of it towered the stout, strong castle of
Nidau, the very personification of the Canton
of Berne. But on the other shore, against the
dark outline of the Jura mountains, the vines
were displayed in all their glory, rows upon
rows of incomparable vines, producing the
best wine in all the world—the best, because
it comes from that beloved spot, where the
dear home was to which my thoughts so
constantly return.

How different was the Bienne of those
days! To-day it is a huge, thriving community
with a population much like other popula-
tions. But then it was a little city all of its
own with its aristocracy both of wealth and
birth. The demi-gods lived apart from us,
romantic and unapproachable in their magnificent houses—a little world in miniature,
far more secure than the world of to-day, for
that was a time when things knew and kept
their "place." How little, though, have I myself changed since those childhood days. I
still only feel comfortable where there is a
" top-dog" and an "under-dog."

Bienne kept Christmas, of course, and the Celebration of the Swiss Republic, but a far more important festival—or at any rate, I found it so—was that of Shrove Tuesday. The whole city would then be positively infested with masks and in the *Neumarktplatz,* or great square, would appear, in all their glory—oh joy of joys!—Leilich and Wallenda and Hipleh and Weiffenbach with their hurdy-gurdies, their portable booths and complement of freaks, complete. My childish soul could scarcely contain itself for the joy thereof.

The very first carnival night I remember in Bienne, Friend Wetzel appeared with his troupe. He called on us and met with a great reception. But the poor fellow was in the depths of depression, declaring that his "orchestra from Geneva" had left him in the lurch. (An "orchestra from Geneva" for a troupe of eleven, all told!)

After he had taken leave of us I crept out after him:

"Couldn't I . . . couldn't I . . . do your music for you?"

"You, Adrien, laddie?"

"Do let me . . ."

GROCK

That selfsame day found me transformed into a substitute for the Genevan orchestra, sitting in the miniature tent in the Neumarktplatz at a regular mincing-machine of a piano, accompanying the Wetzel troupe through their gala programme, with marches, pot-pourris, overtures and what-not, all from memory. I pounded in the bass for all I was worth, in my efforts to drown the hurdy-gurdies shrieking round me. Through my thumping could be heard the raucous tones of the Wallendas' mighty steam organ with its drums, cymbals and percussion, grinding out over and over again the Overture of the Peasant and the Poet. We repeated our show every hour and collected each time a goodly audience of masks and faces. It was a sight for sore eyes to behold the Wetzel family performing on the trapeze or the tight-rope, surrounded by a ring of gaping spectators in the glare of the naptha torches.

My performance on the piano, that caused universal satisfaction, was the outcome of at most nine hours' instruction. I had given about as much time to the study of the violin, while my father had taught me in addition to handle the flute and clarinet. That was my entire musical education. Wetzel wanted to engage me, once his time at Bienne was up, to go with them to Reconvilier, and play there in my native place. Now my father was a very well-balanced man, full of common sense. Most parents would have forbidden anything of the kind, but that is precisely what he did not do. On the contrary, he allowed me to go, and took upon himself sole responsibility for my non-attendance at school.

8

SLEEPLESS NIGHTS AND THE MAGICIAN'S CHEST

AFTER a three days' season in Reconvilier I said farewell to the Wetzel troupe who were faring further afield in the Jura on tour, and returned to Bienne, full of experiences and fuller still of plans for the future. I knew my calling now and what I wanted to be; if need be, I would bite my way through the Alps towards Milan.

A professional friend of mine once saw the great Swiss painter, Hodler, painting the great Niesen mountain by the Lake of Thun in the garden of the Stag Hotel at Gunten. It was on a Sunday afternoon in August and the garden was full of trippers brought thither by the steamboats; they swarmed in their hundreds round his easel, gaping with curiosity, but Hodler painted on with the utmost composure, as though nothing existed in the whole world but himself and his mountain. That is the essential attitude of all those who wish to accomplish anything or who have accomplished anything, it matters not in what walk of life. It is my attitude. I could stand in the great Cathedral Square in Cologne in the full glare of day, smearing my face with a fresh make-up, to the exclusion of all else.

My goal and I were one from the very beginning. My boy's eyes would regard the world simply as a place wherein I might practise my hand-springs and efforts on the tight-rope. Once, when the noonday traffic was at its height, I balanced myself, feet in air, on the bridge-rail in the Bienne Central Square. The river was in full spate with the recent rains. Innumerable passers-by were seized with horror at the inevitable accident that must ensue, and nothing but the technical skill of the future acrobat rescued him from the peril of those two hundred pairs of arms stretched out for his salvation.

On another occasion I proceeded to school by the most natural of routes—the wire fences fronting the little gardens of the houses that line the river bank. At about a yard from the ground I tight-roped along the distance of three quarters of a mile from the lake into the town. I was followed by a bevy of admiring school friends and we all arrived late. Germiquet, the teacher, looked reproachfully at me with his kind eyes, which really hurt almost more than the rap of a cane across one's clenched fist, or being made to kneel with bare knees across this same cane on the ground—both of which punishments were rife in our school. Notwithstanding all of which, a certain innate cocksureness and my unswerving faith in my career-to-be were proof against all reproach and punishment. My father, generous and understanding as ever, paid all necessary fines for non-attendance at class.

Then came a bolt from the blue! One day in November Wetzel drew up in a wagon before our house and asked permission to store with us till the spring half a dozen baskets containing theatre properties and costumes, as he wanted to call in his circus for the winter. You may well believe his request was granted with the utmost alacrity and the baskets stowed away in an outhouse.

Father and Wetzel sat till late together in the bar that evening. I, meanwhile, lay in bed in the attic with eyes wide open, pondering on those baskets and the marvels they contained. I heard Wetzel's departure at a very late hour. I heard the last train come in from Neuchâtel, and the early train puffing out for Basle; I heard the Bienne sirens beginning to hoot, and still I lay, wide awake, with my eternal vision before my eyes of myself, bowing from the boards of a dazzling metropolitan theatre, before a composite and applauding multitude.

Next day, after various abortive attempts, I at length succeeded in raising the lid of one of the baskets, ever so little; greedily did I insert two fingers and pull forth a white peaked cap. I immediately imparted the great secret to my eldest sister, the confidante of all my dreams for the future. Together we tip-toed back to the barn and managed to open the basket lid quite wide, between us. We found a whole collection of caps, white, green and red, together with various dilapidated ruffs and odds and ends of materials. The real magician's chest full of treasures of great price was—need I say it?—the big one underneath all the others, but do as we would, our united efforts were not sufficient to move it.

But we had enough to go on with. We immediately got to work, and by the following Sunday I was sufficiently far advanced to invite my schoolmates to a show in our bar parlour at the back of the inn. I appeared before them in a get-up reminiscent of the rainbow. The programme opened with a "musical bottle turn"; the bottles were filled with varying degrees of water and then struck with a wooden spoon, each bottle, according to the amount of water it contained, giving out a different tone. I played a Bernese march upon them, and the Marseillaise. After which I initiated my audience into the elementary mysteries of the contortionist's craft, and did splits before them. A violin turn, treated acrobatically, and accompanied by my sister in masterly fashion, at the piano, brought the performance to a close amid universal acclamations.

I had made my first public appearance. My father in particular was delighted, and the very next day sent for a list for me of all the big instrument makers and costumiers in Switzerland. Next, he bought me a mandolin. He was smitten with the notion of increasing his public-house custom by means

THAT'S HOW WE LIVED IN SARAGOSSA!

NOW WAS I NOT A BREAKER OF HEARTS?

of my variety turns. So on Sunday I started and repeated my programme before an audience of decidedly appreciative grown-ups. The following Sunday I treated them to a fresh turn in which I helped myself to a meal of spaghetti with my feet. Such enthusiastic encores did this meet with that I was forced to consume a second helping. I went round with the hat in the pauses, and by the end of the month had collected fifteen francs, all told—quite a tidy little sum, but woefully insufficient for the purchase of an acrobat's costume, all bespangled—my dream of dreams.

I found myself unable to possess my soul in patience any longer, and one half holiday I shut myself up in the outhouse with hammer, chisel and screw-driver and the stump of a candle. I then attacked the large chest, tooth and nail. At long last I succeeded in freeing it from its heavy encumbrances, and then . . . *then* . . . I prised upon the mystery of mysteries! My wildest hopes were realised! There they all were, acrobats' kits galore, tights of every hue, caps, wigs, powder-puffs, grease paint, hand mirrors . . . I laid predatory hands upon them all.

71   F

What happened afterwards had to be told me. As the evening drew on and I had not put in an appearance, my family came to look for me. They finally espied the light coming from the outhouse, and, breaking open the door, found me immersed in the great packing case, all amongst the tights and wigs, fast asleep, with powdered face, partially painted with the traditional clown's grin. From that moment the magic treasure house was closed to me.

But the very next day I found something in its place. In one of the biggest shop windows in Bienne a length of glittering stuff had been flaunting ever since Carnival night. I bought three yards of it with the fifteen francs I had collected, and hid it in a place where nobody on earth could find it—in the empty dog kennel beneath the steps.

That dog kennel was my first dressing-room. There I sat, sewing myself an acrobat's costume, and daubing myself with a clown's mouth and red nose. Directly school was over, I sped home like the wind and crept through the round hole into my little refuge; for weeks I got up at five in the morning, and crawling out on to the roof would cling on to

the inn sign and let myself go slithering down
the wall of the house; then, to sew in my dog
kennel till at last the costume was ready and
I could present myself, one memorable evening, before a crowded room, complete in
spangled tights. I twisted myself into the
most amazing attitudes till it was hard to tell
where I ended and where I began. Then I
turned to my instruments and played on my
"Devil's Fiddle," and for my final turn
arrayed myself in my first clown's dress that
also had been cut out and sewn together in
the dog kennel. I had chosen the colours of
the Canton of Berne; yellow, with red and
black stars.

My enthusiasm knew no bounds, and my
efforts at contorting the human body never
ceased. There were days when I would work
for ten hours on end on the trapeze I had put
up behind our house. I took no notice of
either spectators or applause. All I beheld
was the utmost summit of success, attended
by world fame. And on these dizzy heights,
two words twinkled: CIRQUE FERNAN-
DO. That was the greatest circus of all. I
stood, as yet, lurking beneath, in its mighty
shadow.

On one occasion in particular, my father had invited a number of friends to a "cheese fondue." My hour had come. I proceeded to magic the guests. The rich cream cheese put before them began to flame; it turned into coal and then into coke. They stared and stared. My audience included, moreover, a sprinkling of local celebrities, and that night really was a triumph for me. They regarded me as nothing short of a sorcerer. Inanimate objects would change both their weight and their substance so soon as I approached them; they would turn towards me like metal shavings to a magnet, and let me do with them as I would.

9

COMINGS AND GOINGS

At a later stage of my existence, once having become a big "draw," I have been the means of retrieving the fortunes of more than one circus and music-hall. But the fortunes of the "House of Paradise" I could not retrieve. Being an inn outside the town it was a summer resort and did not attract winter customers. My father, too, with his large heart and simple nature, was not the man to look after his own interests. Our departure, however, was not really due so much to the fact of the seasons or my father's professional shortcomings as to some mysterious, inevitable law that ruled the house of Wettach. I know not what to call it. Our settled days were over and the period of unrest had once more arrived. We must needs move from Bienne to the "Stag" (Hotel du Cerf) in Villeret.

Our leave-taking was as depressing and melancholy as our advent had been confident

76

and joyous. It was as though we had a premonition of the years of want and uncertainty that lay before us. Sitting in the train that was bearing us away from old haunts, I held my face firmly pressed against the window-pane, not wishing anyone to see the tears coursing down my cheeks. For the last time I caught a glimpse of the lake as the train rolled over the bridge. A furniture van had already drawn up before the "House of Paradise"; the new landlord was moving in; strange children were already romping on the steps; a black cur of a dog was already messing up the garden, and to his tender mercies would be consigned the kennel, my dressingroom and the cradle, so to say, of my future glory.

No more tight-roping to school! No more mountain expeditions! No more jolly shooting contests amid the vine-clad hills! No more basking in the sunlight on the Jura slopes with the Alps in the distance, stretching from the Tirol right away towards France. One last gaze and the city towers had disappeared into the misty distance, and become a thing of the past.

And now began a kind of life that of all

modes of existence is least suited to Switzerland, that land that sets certitude and solid housekeeping at the head of its cardinal virtues. Our way of living was desultory and devoid of plan. We could not then know it was but a circuitous route leading to the great and desired goal. My sisters, nowadays, lead lives that are sheltered and comfortable. My mother dwells in a nice country house, close to Paris. My father enjoyed a happy and care-free old age. He died in my arms, and on the last day of his life, said this: "You have always been a good son to me."

As a family we invariably clung together, and the worse things went with us, the more united we became. Wherever I was, and whatever I did, be it as far afield as in South America, the thought of my own people was always uppermost in my mind and I was for ever secretly acting on their behalf and in their interests. It's a great thing, this family feeling. It goes a long way to make a man win through. It fortifies him. It gives a man more strength to stand—his own strength and that of the family to which he belongs.

In Villeret, a Jura village of white, chalk-faced houses, lying in its wide valley amidst forest and hills, everything went swimmingly with us at first. The Stag boasted an excellent clientèle, and from my point of view was altogether ideal. I immediately set up a stage in the corner of the bar parlour, and inaugurated concerts without delay, playing regularly every Saturday and Sunday. I posted the four neighbouring villages with bills painted by myself, the first ever to flaunt my name:—

VARIETY ENTERTAINMENT AND CONCERT AT THE STAG INN, PRESENTED BY WETTACH JUNIOR, THE CELEBRATED ARTISTE AND MUSICIAN.

Week by week, every Saturday and Sunday, the room was crowded. That an inn-keeper's son should have the audacity to transform himself into a public acrobat was an unheard-of circumstance in those conservative circles. Friends would come to me telling me what was being said: "Don't miss going to the 'Stag' to see the proprietor's son perform young Wettach; the lad's a marvel!"

One evening after my show, a strapping and jovial individual came up to me: "Bravo, young Wettach . . . Very well done . . ." Whereupon he shook me by the hand till my bones nearly cracked in two. My father knew him and greeted him cordially: "Miseray!" Our visitor was no less than the popular Town Constable from Le Locle.

"Are you on a thief hunt?"

"Better than that. In the wine trade these days. Come on here from Tavannes. Your boy's fame is spreading through the valley. Now I've left the Force to turn innkeeper, I'll engage the rascal for a series of shows in my place at Le Locle."

"All right," quoth I. "But Father and Mother must come too. They can yodel while I play on the Devil's Fiddle."

I don't think I have mentioned the fact that my father was not only a distinguished athlete but also one of the best yodellers of his day. He composed several yodelling songs, one of them especially, "Jodel vom Col des Roches," bringing him much fame. My mother, too, had a very pleasant singing voice, and they would often sing together for their own pleasure and that of all who heard them.

A fortnight later, the Wettach Trio (father, mother and son), appeared for three days with considerable success at Victoria, near Le Locle, the great watchmaking centre in the Neuchâtel mountains. We returned home enriched with a substantial sum in cash and the sympathetic appreciation of many good folk. So much for our beginnings at Villeret.

10

SUSANNA IN THE BATH

I KNOW what I know. I know what it means to have money enough to make money come to you, and even enough to make money stay. But for years on end I lived as poor as a church mouse, and I still think with horror of the days when I had to kow-tow to every scoundrel simply because I had no cash.

It's easy enough to be decent and show character with a bank balance at one's back. Having money improves one's character. Having money means self-assurance, decency and freedom, and I am determined to fight tooth and nail for such freedom. Money isn't just a dead thing. Money is a live entity, a very difficult, elusive and most touchy personage, and whether this entity be great or small—but particularly when small—it needs to be continually assured how greatly you love it, and how impressed with its value you are. I like money and money likes me. I am on "man to man" terms with my salary and no nonsense.

One of the most considerable amounts I ever earned was on my last Swiss tour in Le Locle, La Chaux-le-Fonds and Bienne. I sailed along in my car through that very valley where I had plodded along three and thirty years ago for the first time—oh, with what a difference!

It was in the depths of winter. My shoes gaped with holes, coat I had none, while the ends of my trousers were so ragged they might have been fringed with lace. Under one arm I carried my fiddle, and my wicker basket under the other. Through the valley and through the snow I trudged with an east wind blowing about me that cut like a knife. A Neuchâtel date with the Wetzels had failed completely, the cold being so Arctic that not a soul would venture into the tent. So hungry had we been that when night fell I would nibble the last remnants of frozen cabbage heads from kitchen gardens. An acquaintance advised me to try my luck at the Heidsiek Beer House in St. Imier, a large Jura village. I spent my last penny on a railway ticket and went down the mountain side to Les Geneveys where I alighted and walked the four hours' journey to St. Imier.

Here I worked for the space of three nights, and before I left, old Heidsiek himself bestowed upon me a parting admonishment: "Laddie... Laddie... don't go with acrobats and such"... At Chaux-de-Fonds I may be said to have followed his advice, for I stayed there a whole week and never once climbed a tight-rope or got into fleshings, but hacked wood, pure and simple, for an innkeeper at the rate of two francs a day.

But I am anticipating. I must tell things how they happened, harking back to Villeret where I was a fifteen-year-old youngster, emancipated at last from the rigours—so often evaded—of school attendance. The choice of a sound and respectable means of livelihood had now to be made.

My Father. Well, Adrien, and what would you like to be?

Myself. How should I know? Perhaps a photographer?

My Father. Or a hairdresser?

Myself. Dentist?

My Father. Confectioner?

Myself. Gamekeeper?

My Father. Undertaker?

We laughed. But directly afterwards I became serious. "I want to be something terrific."

"What exactly do you mean by that?"

"I mean I want people to laugh . . . to laugh like anything . . . to simply split their sides whenever they catch a sight of me . . ."

"You might do worse."

I have already told you what a discerning father I had. He knew me through and through and how, once I'd got an idea in my head, all the King's horses and all the King's men couldn't get it out again.

That night I drew up a great Swiss tour with my sister, and a week later off we went together, dancing and singing and doing our little stunts in Berne, then Lucerne, then in a suburb of Zürich, then St. Gall, Schaffhausen, Aaran, Solothurn and Bienne.

My only excuse must be that I really did not realise what I was doing. That knowledge came to me when my Bienne relatives actively protested against the disgrace of a tight-rope walker in the family, and demanded my instant return.

I went back home. Things had meanwhile changed considerably for the worse. Business at the "Stag" was decidedly bad. My father had got work in the watch factory at Malleray, near by. I myself was now placed as apprentice in a watch factory. But sitting still on a workman's bench was not for me. A wine merchant in Tramelan was my next employer. He had just become proprietor of a hotel at a small health resort on the Lake of Geneva. I was the "boy".

The hotel was a small, poky little affair in a village overlooking the lake. It possessed an old-established clientèle that made all advertisement superfluous. It did not even boast an inn sign, but the landlord and landlady supplied this deficiency in their own persons; he, like a mountain of flesh, as substantial as you make 'em, with a head far too small for his body, on which it perched like a great wart, for neck he had none; the landlady was even more massive, with a colossal coiffure of red, hairy snake rings, and blue goggly eyes that made me shiver to look at. When this hefty couple were not sleeping they would be sitting in the office, eating the stodgiest of stodgy food; even their breakfast was served up with meat and potatoes. From the very first moment she couldn't bear

MY PARTNER, ANTONET

ON TOUR IN THE CARPATHIANS

me, probably divining something antago-
nistic in me from the start.

I had smuggled my mandolin up into my
attic room and there I would sit, dreaming
and strumming by the curtained window at
night, often for hours on end. A Saxon lady,
who had seen "better days," presumably
heard my playing, for she came into the coffee
room with a guitar that she asked me to tune
for her. I did so, but no sooner had I left the
coffee room to go to the office than both landlord and landlady pounced upon me with the
question: "You little good-for-nothing—did
we engage you to come here and strum on a
banjo?"

That night I was ordered to heat up my
mistress's bath. In my rage I'd have liked to
sprinkle it with sulphuric acid. But my revenge was otherwise. I went and peeped
through the keyhole instead. For a long time
I could make out nothing but a mass of pink
flesh, bolstery and shapeless. But once the
pink conglomeration had heaved itself into
the bath, sluicing the water furiously over the
edge, I was able to distinguish back from
front and to realise that the red hair was
nothing but a wig, now hanging on a hook!

Her own locks consisted of nothing but a few black rats' tails! My super-Valkyrie was disenchanted for ever in my sight, and I saw I had trembled before nothing but a scarecrow. Enough. I tiptoed away, with a most pleasant sense of vengeance consummated, resolved now to take my own line, and, if necessary, provoke the breach myself.

Next morning, I was staggering from office to coffee room with a pyramid of some forty plates, when the landlord accosted me with orders to clear out that very day, before noon.

"Why?"

"... you dirty Peeping Tom, you ..."

Whether from fright, or of deliberate intent, or in amazement at this sudden notice to quit, I dropped my pyramid of plates! I leave you to believe how devastating was the result, what a clutter and clatter of smashing crockery filled the air!

This disaster cost me my month's salary —not yet paid—as well as my beloved mandolin, that I was forced to pawn and have never yet redeemed. I did not leave till the evening train, for I had yet another reckoning to settle. It was the cashier, an Italian, who had seen me at the keyhole, and given me away. From sheer jealousy! Actually he was enamoured of the freak landlady!

I watched out for the skunk, and when he left the house that evening fell upon him and belaboured him in accordance with all the rules of cudgelling. My opponent was five years older than myself, but anger, and the realisation of my new-won freedom, redoubled my strength.

FATHER AND SON

IT was late on a September evening that I turned up again at home, and then it was that, for the first and last time in his life, my father bestowed upon me the merest ghost of a reproof.

"I don't really know, Adrien, how we're going to feed you . . ."

"Never mind, Dad—you leave that to me . . ."

Next evening I was playing at the Café Wysz in Reconvilier. At the end of three days I had taken 180 francs! I had changed the money into five-franc pieces, thirty-six of them, all brand new, tucked away in my pockets. I said not a word, but was as pleased as anything.

Mother had already gone to bed.

"Well, Adrien, what luck?" Her soft, dubious tones came to me out of her pillows.

"Here's a perfectly good five-franc piece for you, Mother," I answered her, and threw the shining coin on to her counterpane.

"And another of them . . . and another . . ."

"Adrien!!!"

"And another . . . and another . . . and another . . ."

Mother simply couldn't believe it, but lay there speechless, with open mouth. The coins were piled up on her bed, all round her. We laughed hugely, and I was happy as a king.

That very evening I went off to a new job at another good-sized Jura village, near Tramelan. I was to be waiter at the "Stroppa Buffet" with the additional duty of amusing the clients by playing to them on the piano once they had been fed. But once again my pugnacious disposition upset the apple-cart. When I was going round with the plate, late at night, making my collection for the entertainment I alone had provided, a woodcutter fellow, sitting alone at a table, a most evil-looking customer, got up and dotted me one, for no reason whatever. The plate was knocked out of my hand, and fell in pieces on the floor, while the money rolled around the room. I let it roll, and went for my opponent, landing him one under the chin so successfully that he staggered backwards, tumbled down, cursing, and broke his arm. On which he was removed to the Bienne hospital.

My good job ended simultaneously.

Next day I ran into my father at Tavannes, quite by chance. He looked infinitely woebegone when I broke it to him that I must again be on the look out for work.

"You never seem able to stick it out . . . You're like a bluebottle in a closed room, banging against all the window panes . . ."

"Yes, but Dad, when a fellow hits you on the right cheek, do you ever turn the left?"

"Don't talk nonsense."

"But I tell you . . ." And I proceeded to relate what had happened to me in Tramelan. The old boy became as heated as I was myself by the end of the story. He clapped me on the shoulder, shouting: "Good lad! That's the stuff to give 'em!" over and over again.

"Go on as you've begun, my boy; when they give you a black eye you give 'em two, and if you don't get away with it—why, send for me, and I will! See?"

He shook me by the hand, treated me to another sausage and beer, and we parted the best of friends. He took the train to Malleray and I to Bienne.

I turned my longing eyes towards the dear old place as we thundered over the bridge. It was good to catch a glimpse of old haunts. All the same, I made a considerable detour, in order to avoid past memories, on my way to my new job in Meylan's Beer House in Marktgasse, a street in a very poor neighbourhood, where I was to be dish-washer and lamp cleaner at a wage of twenty francs per month. I stayed there a couple of months, then went on to the Metropole, and then to another pot-house, since defunct, in the Kanalgasse. But I will not bore my readers further with my beery peregrinations through half Switzerland. One good thing, at any rate, resulted from my stay in Bienne, and that was running into a former school friend, my dear and excellent pal Joram Liegme, whom I persuaded to go on tour with me round about Basle and across into Alsace.

But at Basle we were hauled up, willy-nilly, before local authority, in the shape of a police official with an eye-glass and falsetto voice, who shrilly reprimanded us and had us shut up in the town gaol for daring to appear in a suburban café without a performer's licence. Our tour ended with a jerk, and we travelled, ticketless, by rail—do you remember those old days, Joram?—to an uncle and aunt in Reconvilier, our fellow passengers making a collection on our behalf when the guard came to take the tickets and wanted to run us in!

Joram Liegme runs the Hotel Jerusalem, these days, in La Chaux-de-Fonds. I could hardly refrain from crying when, two years ago, in the midst of my amazingly successful Swiss tour, I visited him and he gathered his children around me, declaring to them with the utmost pride:

"Take a good look at him now. That's Grock . . . the famous Grock . . . But he and I worked together when he was still Wettach!"

12

A CHAPTER OF LAW AND ORDER

GROCK the Famous! But how easily it might have been Grock the Infamous! I imagine there are few honourably-minded men with hot blood in their veins who have not been in danger, at some time or another in their lives, of sinking down into that world where the ordinary rules of law and order are unrecognised. I come of a hot and heady stock and the blood of my ancestors frequently runs riot in my veins. I shall never know how many crazy impulses that otherwise might have led me straight to the police courts, I have worked off on my little trapeze bar. As a newly-breeched infant I remember lying in my bed and overhearing my grandmother say one night to my mother:

"That boy will make himself felt in the world by hook or by crook. Mark my words, it will be one way or another. If it's a good way, then it will be a very good way, if bad, then bad all through!"

It is a matter of constant wonder to me how I, despite all the traps and pitfalls I have had to encounter, have ended by becoming the more or less useful member of society whom you behold to-day.

There was a time when it was a very near thing! That was at La Chaux-de-Fonds, in a very lean year, when my family's prospects were even more serious than usual. It was then I got to know young B., one of the slickest acrobats, and one of the oddest human creatures I have ever encountered. The youth positively had nothing solid in his make-up; he was simply a piece of flexible muscle to be contorted into any shape required. No crack or cranny was too minute for him to slip through; the last I heard of him he had been run in for breaking open the till in the booking office of the Bienne railway station, which place he had entered by slithering down the chimney. He did time for it, but that was many years ago. Since then I have heard no more, but I can't somehow believe he is either dead or in gaol. He would always escape from any prison you put him in, and has not yet slipped even into the devil's clutches, I should say.

We read in certain romantic books of human beings unlike ordinary mortals, a sort of betwixt and between creation, if I may put it that way. They are of no definite age, and although ubiquitous, are never to be caught. He was such a creature.

It was his very uncanniness attracted me. We would be walking along the street together, for instance, talking. All of a sudden I would realise he was no longer there. To whom had I just been speaking? Or else he would suddenly be walking alongside me in a brand-new overcoat, when I knew perfectly well that a moment before he had had no coat on at all! He was absolutely indifferent and completely detached. His eyes were devoid of any expression; they were merely two sockets filled with water of a greyish green. His hands would be chilly on the sultriest summer day. I still shudder thinking of a night I spent in the same bed with him. If I so much as touched his naked skin it was both cold and damp.

Through its constant repetition I began to notice something that at first had escaped me. On certain days even his fish's tempera-

ture would seem to rise. He would seem to
be trembling inwardly, and his eyes would
be red-rimmed. These red-rimmed eyes
were inevitably the prelude to his sudden re-
appearance, after an interval of some hours,
with money in his pockets, new shoes, a new
tie, smart walking stick, watch, and on one
occasion with a gold-handled pen-knife. One
day it suddenly dawned on me that B. was
nothing more nor less than a common thief.
I didn't tell him I knew it, but I wanted to
break away from him that instant without
his knowing. But I couldn't; whether it was
his cold-bloodedness, his calm criminality
or his perpetually challenging attitude to
danger, his mysterious personality continued
to fascinate me.

One day, in Bienne, B. bought himself a
pair of tights, in my company, for ten francs
—of course, stolen. The shop was in a small
side street, owned by an old lady. He also
wanted, he told her, a cardboard box, of such
and such a length and such and such a
breadth—and he named the most amazing
proportions. The old lady looked for one in
vain, and finally said she thought she had
something in her cellar that might suit him.

"Good. My friend here will help you look for it."

Nothing loth, I went with the old lady down into her cellar. She found what she wanted and we emerged once more into the shop, when B. hastily said good-day and we left together. Meanwhile, without my having any idea of it, he had profited by our absence to steal a packet of handkerchiefs. Two hours later we were both of us arrested, confronted with the stolen goods and hailed off to the police station.

Next day we were brought before the Magistrate who ordered fourteen days' imprisonment for B. and for me a fine of twenty francs as his accomplice.

I was actually written down as a thief's accomplice! In spite of my complete and utter innocence I was both fined and acclaimed as the accomplice of a thief!

To-day I am Grock the famous clown, whose mere name suffices to pack theatres all over the world with all kinds of people, simple folk as well as intelligentsia; they crowd in, one and all, to see and hear me, and no sooner do I wamble on to the stage with my chair and trunk, than highbrows and lowbrows are convulsed to a man. I perform the best of all possible tasks, for I spread mirth and merriment around me wherever I go and no one is gladder than I am to be able to do it. But I wonder, shall I be believed when I tell you that sometimes, even now, in the midst of all these plaudits, the old conviction of injustice suffered sometimes comes over me? I would like, when this happens, to rip off the lid of my piano and smash it into pieces. Rage seizes me by the throat to such an extent that I could rush then and there from the footlights and plant the red flag on the roof of every prison and police court in the world. Oh, I can understand only too well how the world could well go crazy from this sense of insufferable wrong! Of course I know I have little, if any, personal right to get all worked up like this. My life has revenged my injuries long ago. What is my little grievance, compared with the injustice suffered by millions of men for which they will never be requited? Nevertheless, this youthful experience of mine continues to rankle right up to this present day.

It has involved me in the discussion of that most ticklish of all problems—what is

Justice? What is right and what is wrong? In my quieter moments of reflection I ask myself whether perhaps it was not my "old Adam," or whatever you choose to call it, that was undergoing punishment that day, rather than the actual deed? I have even got to the pitch, these days, of being able to regard this piece of gross injustice as a kind of payment against my considerable amount of original sin, and accepting it as such without too much botheration.

But of what use are these subtleties to a child who feels himself guiltless from top to toe? Here I stood in all my innocence, as clear to me as was the summer's sun, but the sun was no good. Here I was confronted with utter blindness, and all the sheer stupidity of office, and could do nothing against them. It was that made me see red. I suddenly realised how little the things counted by which I had been wont to set most store. I knew now that my right to live only existed in so far as I could fight for it with my own fists. And that conviction still lingers on in me.

Relatives advised me: "tie a stone round your neck and walk into the lake": acquaint-

BUENOS AIRES, 1907

ALMOST COURT JESTER TO THE SULTAN, CONSTANTINOPLE, 1907

ances cut me. The utmost down-and-outs seemed to avoid me. I was an outcast, a pariah. It was touch and go that I did not start from that moment to slide rapidly downhill. But my "spring-mattress temperament" rose to the occasion. However hard they might try to press me down, up I rose once more. In fact the harder a mattress is pressed, the more bounce there is in it. I waited an opportunity to show the world I still knew how to bounce—and the opportunity soon came.

13

A TIGHT-ROPE ESCAPADE

My people were back again in Bienne, living in a little place in the centre of the town. There was a crisis in the watch-making trade, times were bad and prospects far from rosy. Father was out of work again. Any job I tried to do was a dead failure, whether it were addressing envelopes, acting as messenger boy or as cook's boy in a hotel: it was no good; the story of my thieving had got about everywhere.

One evening, after sunset, I was walking aimlessly outside the town when I saw a solitary pedestrian coming towards me, a little thin, frail man with the hesitating, irresolute gait of a badly-made puppet. I recognised him as the Magistrate, but he had no notion who I was, as he walked past me in his namby-pamby way with one fleeting glance from beneath his big, rimmed glasses. But the look of hate and venom that I bestowed on him was such as to make him start and then hasten his steps.

I set my teeth and followed him. I scarcely knew myself for the rage that was in me. Not a soul was about. The park we were in was as lonely, as lonely as could be. "Do him in," something in me was crying out, "*do him in;* no one's looking; he'll be the last person able to say anything." The distance between us was diminishing rapidly; I could hear my arch-enemy coughing . . . one moment more and I should be up with him . . . treading on his heels . . .

Our way lay over a bridge. What a chance! But another pedestrian coming to meet us, brought me to my senses. I stopped short, trembling from head to foot. The magistrate disappeared into the shadow of the rocks.

"Hallo . . . if it isn't Wettach! Why, I've been looking for you all over the place!"

Louis Bourquin was standing looking at me, a tight-rope walker and athlete of great repute in our town.

"I've got a licence to tight-rope in the Square and want a partner to work with. You're the only one who could do it. Wherever have you been hiding? For days I've been trying to find you. Why, what's the matter with you, old man?"

I leant against the bridge, staring at him.
He went on: . . . "I to dance on the tight-rope
and you to do stunts on the stage beneath.
Would five francs be all right for you?"

"Bourquin . . . you're rotting . . ."

He rummaged in his pockets and produced
the police permit that he held under my
nose.

"Now d'you believe it?"

"Yes . . . yes . . . oh, yes . . ."

I went quite dizzy. Suddenly the world
had become an entirely different world. What
a chance for getting my own back! Now the
whole town should see what I could do and
who I was. I tore down the hill with Bourquin. By the light of a little lantern we practised in the playing fields outside the city
every handspring and contortion we could
think of, till midnight came and went.

It was towards the end of May. The afternoon had been close with the first thunderstorm of summer, but the evening was cool
and calm. Long before the time due for our
performance to begin, a crowd had collected
in the Square, attracted by our preparations
in open daylight. The news had gone all

round the town. Already a rope had been stretched right across the Square from the third storey of the Schweizerhof Hotel to the third floor window of the Café de Jura. There were lights in all the houses, and all the windows were filled with peering heads. At the eleventh hour we found we were unable to use the safety net; it was too rotten to be of any good. Bourquin must perform on his rope without one. Within the little match-board dressing-room we had knocked up for ourselves, he started to talk to me. He had already got into his green-spangled tights, and was trembling in every limb :

"I can't do it . . . I tell you I simply *can't* . . . I'm in the most utter funk . . . something awful . . . You'll have to go!"

"Let's draw lots for it."

We did, and I won. It was up to me now to negotiate that rope without a net.

I picked up the great, heavy balancing pole, walked across the Square into the Schweizerhof and up the staircase into the third floor room. I can still see that room to-day, just a common or garden hotel room with heavy, plush furniture, and a couple of

coloured prints hanging on the walls, one of
the German Emperor and Empress, the
other of Victor Emanuel of Italy, not the
present monarch but the old one, *Il Re
Galantuomo*. Quite a number of people
were already in the room; they received me
in dead silence, and I had the feeling they
would have liked to have said something,
but could not. But suddenly someone
rushed up the stairs after me and seized me
by the arm.

"Are you crazy ... d'you want to break
your neck?"

I was perfectly calm, both inwardly and
outwardly, and was thinking quite coolly of
what to do in the event of my nerve failing
on the rope so that I lost my balance. I decided I would fling down my balancing pole
and cling to the rope like grim death. If
the pole broke human heads in transit, I
could only hope they would be those of
rascals who deserved it.

I climbed out on to the window-sill and
looked down upon the Square in the light
cast by a ring of petroleum lamps. It was
thronged with expectant heads. Cockchafers
were dashing themselves against the lamps,

attracted by their light.

"Hold tight for all you're worth," I adjured the two assistants who were posted, one each end of the rope. These youths were white with anxiety, and one of them already so overcome, his knees gave way beneath him and he must perforce sit down.

Now for it! With all the resolution at my command, I gulped down a sudden sense of terror and, stretching out my pole in front of me, placed both feet upon the rope, and stood, balancing. I can still smell the scent of jasmin, from the neighbouring garden! In fact, from that day to this I have never liked the scent of that flower; jasmin for me always forebodes catastrophe.

All around me stretched the roofs in the clear starlight. The thunderstorm of the afternoon was still rumbling in the distance, and I had the odd experience, due to my strung-up frame of mind, of realising *afterwards* a glimpse I had registered of a far away spire lit by a momentary flash of lightning. A buzzing cockchafer struck me plump on my cheek. But by now I had got a firm command over myself.

Swift and sure, one foot after another, I

had reached the middle of the rope. I could feel the sympathy of my audience all around me, and I was possessed with a feeling of *lightness;* I felt light as a feather, and scarcely even sensed the touch of the rope on my feet. Like a sleep-walker I continued on my perilous way, with a sense of poise so acute it could be hardly called of the body alone, for it included a sense of harmony with the entire world, and I was filled with a feeling of ecstasy I had never known before.

But it was in this very moment of supreme self-control that I overreached myself and dared too greatly, for instead of making my way straight to the goal ahead of me I attempted to turn in the middle.

A murmur of apprehension arose from below. Something, evidently, was going wrong. The rope was beginning to sag, ever so little. The windows all round the Square seemed full of nothing but gaping mouths of horror.

It was sagging more now, and more! Here, a moment before was I, feeling enraptured with the entire world, and in a twink all has changed, and I can only wonder wildly . . . *where* am I . . . WHO am I . . . Everything gets dizzy around me . . . I totter and sway, with frantic aimless gestures of my balancing pole in the air. Quiet now . . . quiet . . . Here I am . . . Here I am . . . am . . . am . . . All the same, the world is dissolving in pieces . . . I get a confused impression of the crowd beneath me rushing in all directions for safety . . . anywhere, so as to avoid me, falling. A window pane is smashed. Someone utters a raucous cry. All resolves itself into hubbub . . . lights, houses, trees, everything whizzing round.

I meanwhile am clinging frantically to my rope with both hands. If you can't cling fast to your rope—why then, you're no tight-rope walker and never will be!

Steady now . . . steady. Slowly and surely, inch by inch, I pull myself along the rope, with my audience below shouting like mad, the nearer I get to the hotel window. Once there, four stout arms are stretched out over the sill to drag me into safety. I am nearly stifled with joyful caresses. They all swarm up the stairs, and I am carried shoulder-high, by utter strangers as well as friends, across the Square, the hero of this most fantastic night.

14

CAPER-CUTTING

Next morning I awoke with a tremendous sense of retaliation accomplished and final re-instalment. It would not have surprised me if the magistrate had arrived in person, complete in top-hat and frock-coat, on a propitiatory call, to beg my pardon and promise a public retraction of my sentence in all the papers! But alas for a dull and uninspired world. My short-lived triumph survived but for a few days; schoolboys nudged one another and stood gaping when I passed by, but otherwise nothing was changed; once again the door shut upon me, and I, the pariah, stood without.

My salvation arrived with an unexpected engagement at Chaux-de-Fonds. Unfortunately by the end of the third day, the boss ran away with the till. I and a pal trailed through all the little villages as far as St. Imier, trying to make money, but in no way succeeding. I made an excursion, one day,

from St. Imier out to Villeret, where I called
in at the "Stag" and was filled with melancholy at the recollection of those old days,
anxious solicitude for my family, and a sense
of my own impotence.

Late in the evening I made my way back
through the valley to St. Imier. The Jura
mountains, with their forests of firs, made the
night darker than ever. How quiet it was. I
began talking softly to myself, a conversation that grew louder as I went on, till I
finished by positively yelling aloud. They
were curses I yelled out into the night. I
cursed myself, the whole of humanity, and
the world in its entirety; the dark stretches
of woodland on either side of me resounded
with the echoes thereof.

I reached St. Imier at midnight only to
learn that my partner had skedaddled, taking my fiddle with him. So that was that!

To stay in my room was impossible. I
should either have smashed all the furniture
to smithereens, or murdered all the occu-
pants of every floor. I rushed from house
and village, through the fields into the forest,
forcing my way through bush and under-

wood, with the boughs scratching my cheeks.

I stumbled downhill, tripping up over the roots of trees, sousing through swamps from which I scrambled by the aid of friendly branches. Still I panted, on and on. My coat and trousers were badly torn, my hat had long since vanished. When I finally emerged from the forest into a meadow I had no more strength left. I flopped on to the ground like a sack, and promptly went to sleep.

My awakening was gentle and gradual. To the feeling of a soft, warm caress, I opened my eyes. I was enveloped in a delicious sense of warmth, followed by something touching my cheek like a piece of damp, and rather rough, velvet. In my astonishment I made a brusque movement. On which a monster sprang back in front of me!

It was actually a cow that was the cause of this tender disturbance from my slumbers—a superb specimen of a piebald, Freiberg cow. She now proceeded, with much satisfaction, to lick her own chops with the tongue that had served to caress me. It was already broad daylight. I had been sleeping in a cow pasture. And there stood the cow contemplating me with adorable, stupid eyes, in such a friendly fashion I must needs burst out laughing.

On which she began to moo, and this primitive note of my own homeland recalled me finally to reality. I got up, feeling solid earth once again beneath my feet, and a clear head on my shoulders. As ragged and dishevelled as any tramp, I clambered down once more into the village and there, at the public house, was presented with a telegram. It was from Bienne and read "Come at once; foreign trip. Mother."

Kissed by a cow in a Jura meadow at early morning, arriving at Bienne by noon, departure thence by five o'clock, swept through the Arlberg tunnel at midnight on my way to Budapest—surely that was the most eventful day of my whole existence? It appeared that one Count Bethlen had advertised for a Swiss private tutor to reside at his country estate at Maros Gesze. My mother had answered and her reply been favourably received, the money for my fare having been sent forthwith, together with a request for my immediate departure. It was all done in such a hurry that I hardly knew if I were on my head or my heels.

My sister, too, had got a situation in a Budapest family as nursery governess. We went off together, aged seventeen and fifteen, respectively, with four francs in our pockets. The previous night I had been rushing with maledictions through the Jura valley. And now, here I was, in the Vienna train!

Innsbruck, Linz, Vienna! Next night we were speeding through Hungary. Early in the morning my sister waked me, pointing out of the window, and, perched on a hill, in the midst of a solitary expanse, I saw a white and ghostly cathedral glimmering in the first sun's rays. The Cathedral of Gran, so a peasant told us.

Budapest! My sister was met there, and I got into another train bound for the "Siebenburgen." On we went in the evening twilight, through a sea of cornfields. Here we were at last at Maros Gesze. A wagonette with four horses was waiting in the station yard, and a youth, about my own age, attended by a manservant, came up to me, holding out his hand and saying: "Good evening, Herr Wettach. My name is Kalman Bethlen."

My trunk was hoisted in and we were soon galloping along the dusty high road, amid the sea of cornfields, still, towards my new friend's home. I sat behind in solitary state, the young Count driving—a dashing and spirited lad for all his slender physique—with the coachman beside him on the box. My young charge, I thought to myself, had just the right make-up for a contortionist. I'd soon teach him to slip his head between his legs and tie himself into knots. Far better than any amount of French lessons!

It was night when we arrived at our destination. We heard the sound of the dogs baying, and as we drove up servants appeared on the steps of the ancestral home, carrying lanterns, while an elderly figure advanced to meet us, a stocky, benevolent-looking individual, with yellow-grey beard and moustache—the old Count. I leapt from the wagonette by means of a somersault, and stood before him, bowing.

For a moment he stood gazing at me in astonishment, then with a smile he removed the stump of a cigar from between his lips, and held out his hand to me, saying:

"My dear young friend, is that how all you Swiss behave?"

"Well ... some of us do, sir ..."

RUSSIA, 1913

IN PETERSBURG

15

UPSIDE DOWN ON A CHIMNEY-POT

How good a thing it is for a human being to have someone over him on whom he can depend for protection as well as commands.

I know the aristocracy to-day is at a discount now that we are all hag-ridden by the slogan of equality. I admit, moreover, that your aristocrat often abuses his position, and the whole ideal of him becomes distorted. But Maros Gesze was the ideal patriarchal establishment.

My feeling for what is right and proper for each and all of us is so acute as to amount, almost, to a sixth sense. I can assure you that this sense was never once offended in Maros in the least degree. On the contrary, that pariah feeling of the outcast that had irked me to desperation so lately in Switzerland, thawed into nothingness at the end of a few days. *Noblesse oblige!* Here, everybody, manservant and maidservant, villager, gamekeeper, steward, tutor, or son and heir, both felt and knew the justness and the rightness of their several stations, and with pleasure submitted to inherited authority in the person of their Father Bethlen. A perfect harmony reigned within this world in miniature.

Oh, blessed land of Hungary! Here we dwelt amid a superfluity I had never so much as imagined, a wealth of good things regarded all as a matter of course. The groaning table at meal times made an unforgettable impression on a creature like myself, so accustomed to the pangs of hunger! I was never tired of retailing these delicacies in my letters home. "Only imagine what we had for dinner, to-day . . . roast boar! Do any of you know what pickled venison is like? We have sausages here, galore, and yesterday a 'Gulasch'! To say nothing of salads, vegetables, fruits and cakes!"

My table companions naturally could not help noticing my appetite. In any other country it would have been received—to say the least of it—with ironical comment, but here they revelled in it; from the Count to the servants, all were genuinely delighted; the dishes would be brought round to me again and again, and when for very shame's sake I felt compelled at long last to refuse, old Miklos, who had stood beaming upon me throughout the ceremony, in his most encouraging fashion, would come whispering into my ear:

"One more helping, Herr Adrien . . . just one more . . ."

"I simply mustn't . . ."

"Oh, just one *little* bit now, Herr Adrien . . . only one!"

By degrees I was able to be myself, naked and unashamed. No need now for the acrobat and contortionist to practise his craft on the sly in secluded spots, especially as my "pupils" had shown themselves positively enchanted the first time they had caught sight of my tricks. Though as yet I was not willing to let them into the secrets of my past, and replied to all their somewhat disconcerting questions with the bare statement, calculated to nip all further enquiries in the bud: "Tumbling is an ancient folk custom in Switzerland!"

As far as my charges were concerned, I was really not engaged so much to teach them a foreign language as to talk French with them in friendly fashion; a relationship that suited nicely with the fact that we were much of an age. Both the youthful Counts were the first to admit my superiority in the field of games. A few weeks' practice had made me an excellent tennis player, and it was in this connexion I made the acquaintance of a cousin of the two brothers, who later became the Hungarian Prime Minister, Bethlen.

A few weeks after my arrival I went with my new friends to the neighbouring town of Maros-Vásárhey. The holidays were over. While the Bethlen brothers were riveted to the benches of their scholastic academy, I would indulge in sabre practice or horizontal and parallel bars in the gymnasium. After school hours we would all play football together in the playing-field outside the town. Here was erected a sugar factory with an enormous high chimney. Why I mention this detail will soon appear.

A bevy of youngsters used to join in our sport. Among them was a certain young Count Szecheny—if I have got the name right—a great rival of mine in sport and still more in the good graces of two charming

young ladies, related to the Bethlen family,
who invariably looked on at our games, and
whose disturbing presence did much to egg
us on to deeds of derring-do. One of these
young ladies was of an ardent disposition,
the other dove-like and reserved. I was
horribly susceptible to the charms of both,
and believed myself, moreover, to be Cock
of the Walk.

One particular day we were all vying with
one another to the top of our bent, on the
football field. The team captained by me
had won three times running. The ladies
were loud in their applause. Szecheny, leader
of the defeated team, was white with rage,
and said not a word. At length he could
contain himself no longer, and strode towards me, pointing to the factory chimney.

"Well—there's one thing you couldn't do,
Herr Adrien, for all you're so clever . . ."

"And that is . . .?"

"Climb up that chimney pot . . ."

"Right you are. I'll do better than that.
I'll stand on my hands on the edge of it."

"Oho! Saying's not doing!"

The challenge had been uttered for all to
hear. The presence of my adored ones made

me stick at nothing. On the outer wall of
the chimney were iron clamps, spaced evenly
all the way up, the first of them a man's
height from the ground. One swing upwards
and I was on the first rung of the ladder.
"Monsieur Adrien . . . Monsieur Adrien . . ."
wailed the young damsels in their dismay . . .
That egged me on like anything, and, clinging on like mad, I began my perilous ascent.
First ten rungs, then twenty were behind
me. . . . Hills I had never so much as seen
hove their gigantic bulk above the horizon,
far away. . . .

The clamps seemed spaced devilishly far
the one from the other. The strain of it was
something awful. About half-way up all the
spirit oozed out of me. My muscles seemed
suddenly made of nothing but pulp. I tauten
up, fight down a strong feeling of giddiness
and clamber on with a hectically beating
pulse. Endless fields of maize spread themselves out before me, waving in the sunshine,
and country estates are dotted all around
with their huge parks like green islands. The
sun is simply scorching. The iron clamps
feel hot to the feet. On I go, panting and
gasping, with the blood hammering away in

my temples. I get giddier and giddier the nearer I get to the summit. The sky above my head quivers like a jelly. One more now . . . and one more . . . And at last I am clinging desperately to the top of the chimney pot!

From it emerges a soft, smoky cloud through which I obtain a blurred vision of the world below. But not more blurred nor muzzy than I feel myself. I can see the church tower of Maros-Vásárhey gleaming in the distance. I feel decidedly uncomfortable. Down below stand my pals and the young ladies in deathly silence. I can see Szecheny's malicious face, without really seeing it. No, my lad, this shall not be your day out! With a sudden movement, I swing myself up on to the chimney pot edge that is about the width of a window sill. So giddy am I, I have to clutch at the lightning conductor for support. Down below, they are all gesticulating like mad for me to come down. But we haven't finished yet—oh, no!

With a shout I plunge down on to my two hands and am poised head downwards, according to promise, my feet just touching

the lightning conductor. The round, black crater of the chimney yawns in front of me. How it smokes . . . how it stinks . . .

Done! Once more I set my two feet deliberately on the chimney's brink and, triumphant and exhausted, begin my descent.

16

A CELEBRATION AND A BOAR HUNT

My feat of bravado had made me tremendously popular, and I came to be regarded as a veritable magician when I set to and repaired a dilapidated and long-given-up violin belonging to one Schmidt, who kept a music shop in Maros-Vásárhey. One day, the President of the Bicyclists' Association called at the house, and invited me, in the most flattering terms, to assist at the celebration of one of their anniversaries: "Without you no beanfeast could be other than a failure!" I asked Count Bethlen for permission to go: he gave it to me with evident amusement, together with ten gulden and his blessing.

And, to speak truth, I am bound to admit that I was the success of the evening. They had set up a little stage in the park and on it I performed, on my own, a programme devoted to music and acrobatics. One item in particular, towards the close of the afternoon, delighted all and sundry. A smartly dressed cyclist, obviously more than half seas over, made his appearance, complete in top-hat, frock-coat and white gloves. He was a peculiarly skilled performer on the bicycle who, despite his quibsy condition, always saved himself from disaster at the last minute. The police immediately ordered him off, as a public menace. But his only reply was to make a long nose at them.

There was nothing left now for injured authority but to mount their cycles and pursue. Five policemen charged furiously after the delinquent who, in less time than it takes to tell, would turn on his tracks and shoot past them with a whoop of delight. The onlookers fairly revelled in it. At length I had had all I could stand of it, and dismounted. Somehow or other I succeeded in explaining to officialdom that I was not really tipsy, and it had all been nothing but a joke. To the delight of all present, the police showed up as excellent sportsmen and enjoyed the joke as much as anybody. I turned up again at my employer's with a copy of Monday's newspaper containing a glowing report of my marvellous exploits, and thereby won the approbation I most valued—that of the Count himself. A special bottle of wine was brought up and drunk to my health.

As for the sport that now came my way! We accounted for eighty hares once, on one day. I rode the horse appropriated to my use, Lila, a magnificent, most unruly beast. How unruly this mare was I didn't know at first; I had approached her with all the air of an expert, though never before had I known what it was to cross a horse. "You can ride, can you not, Herr Adrien?" they had asked me.

"Can I not!"

No sooner was I up than I was down again, lying in the mud with everyone guffawing around me. But now the laugh was to turn against Lila, for when she attempted to throw me a second time I held her like a vice between my thighs and, buck as she would, no centaur could have been more inexorably moulded into her back than was I.

I even had a wild sow to my credit, and am not a little proud of that fact. The old brute was laying waste the peasants' maize fields, and no hunt had so far been able to run her down. One morning a peasant started to complain to me of his misfortunes:

"I've seen the old swine, Monsieur, and she's as big as a baby elephant. I know where she goes to water of an evening, and that's the time to get a pot shot at her."

I crept into the house, selected a gun from the gun-room and surreptitiously followed the man. We came to a pool, about twenty-five metres across, and hid in the reeds. Hours passed, the afternoon crept on, the sun tinged the distant mountains, a village church clock struck six, and then seven, and still no sow—not a sign of her. Hullo! Suddenly a noise like an approaching steam engine, and a whirl of dead leaves among the reeds. There she goes!

I was all of a tremble. My heart was in my mouth. I peeped through the rushes on either side of me, and there was the long awaited monster, alone in all her glory, straight out of the Ark of Noah, with enormous yellow tusks. The moment the beast lowered her head to drink, I fired. And hit! The sow was writhing her head into the muddy swamp. We hurried up and were just in time to glimpse the brute's hindquarters and tail, so deep had she burrowed into the ground in her death agony.

The peasant hurried back to the village for assistance. Three of us together pulled out our prize and loaded it, with many a groan, on to an ox cart. The peasants guessed its weight at six hundred pounds at least. The head alone would have made a good sized animal. We transported our load, four oxen strong, to village and château. There I stood, the hero of the hour, leaning on my rifle against my "bag" and waving to the peasants' acclamations. The noise of it brought the Count out of doors.

"I'm bringing you the wild beast that's been laying waste your property, Count."

Next day the carcass was broken up to the last bristle. The Count had the head stuffed and hung up in the hall, and there my trophy hangs to this day, unless the moths have eaten it.

17

GROCK AS NURSEMAID

I AM no dreamer. Contemplation was never my strong suit. This Garden of Eden kind of life at Maros Gesze was too placid and care-free for me, and when one day I realised my old collar measurement of thirty-seven had grown too small for me, neither God nor all His angels could keep me where I was. The city of Budapest, mighty and meaty, was beckoning me to come.

My family, meanwhile, were installed in Hungary. Six weeks after my departure they had sold up every stock and stool and followed us. Both my small sisters were at school at Budapest. My mother was working in the house of a certain chemist named Tauffer, an excellent fellow, with whose family we became great friends. Father had a job in the great watch factory at St. Gotthard.

But, as usual, my optimism was running ahead of facts. Not one single job could I find, though I looked all day long and every day. One morning I sat myself, exhausted, on a bench in front of the Opera House. Oh, you succulent flesh pots of Maros Gesze, sausages, geese and game, why did I, poor idiot, desert you? Even cigarettes, my usual last refuge, were lacking . . . cigarettes, those precious stimulators of ideas. Next moment I had caught sight of a trickle of smoke from a cigarette stub on the pavement. In a trice I had picked it up and dissected it, and purchased some cigarette paper for two kreuzer, my sole remaining capital; never did any cigarette taste better or give rise to better thoughts.

The world of inanimate objects has always been friendly towards me. Malicious I have never found them. Years ago I was in Barcelona when an anarchist wanted to blow up a café with a bomb. The bomb was placed beneath my chair. I could sniff the lighted fuse, and, groping under my seat, I picked up the abortion, that promptly began to purr like a cat and quite forgot to go off. I have only to walk across a market-place for all the apples to begin to jump about in their baskets, so that the market women

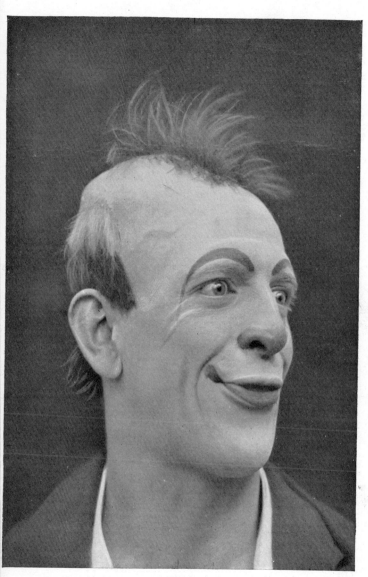

1906

WITH ANTONET IN BERLIN IN 1911

have to guard them from being jostled and juggled by me. I was notorious with the market women in Bienne. So soon as these Amazons caught sight of me they would stand truculently in front of their precious baskets.

A friend of mine lives in the Ticino in lodgings, beneath an old furniture shop, every room of which has an old clock on its chimney-piece, dusty, decrepit, and perfectly silent. I have only got to go and stay with him, and hey presto! the very first night every clock in the establishment starts ticking and striking like mad! Old, discarded pianos thrum audibly when I enter the room they stand in; such a thing actually happened to me in Hungary. I have only to appear in their midst for the ladies of the neighbourhood to increase the population, as on that memorable occasion in Spain. Baron von Münchhausen told tall stories, but Grock does nothing of the kind; Grock is a Münchhausen against his inclination who, willy-nilly, has a peculiar effect upon the world of things, that leads to happenings and consequences.

But to get back to that cigarette end by

the Budapest Opera House; never has the good Spirit of Tobacco worked more rapidly upon me . . . Why, of course, *I had my fiddle!*

I rushed back to my lodging, took the fiddle under my arm, and for the space of a whole week kept my head above water, playing and singing around blocks of tenement flats. One day I went into the nearest music shop to buy some fresh strings. An Italian customer was being served who could not speak Hungarian or make himself in any way understood till I interpreted in French. As I revealed in my remarks a whole stock of technical knowledge where instruments were concerned, Sternberg, the proprietor of the shop, suddenly offered me a dual job— that of his apprentice in the instrument trade, and teacher of French to his children! I took it on.

The Sternbergs were an altogether praiseworthy and useful family. I saw the three brothers the last time I played in Budapest, and they had all made good. It was a family run on typically Jewish lines; no extravagance and no waste; everything economically organised, with a view to getting

on. I learnt a great deal in the workshop
from a very clever workman from Vienna,
Franz Stahl. I had it all at my finger ends
at the end of a few months, the ordinary and
necessary technique of felt renewing, and the
tuning and cleaning of instruments. I also
acquired a complete repairer's outfit that
later accompanied me everywhere. It has
stood myself and others in good stead on
many an occasion, and I should say that in
certain districts of Hungary and Spain it
would be hard to find an antiquated piano
that has not been tinkered up and tuned by
Grock.

One day Sternberg dismissed the nursemaid and I was transplanted from my bed-
room to the nursery, that henceforth I had
to share with three little boys aged three,
nine and ten. I was promoted to be nursery-
maid!

I used to sleep on the sofa. The alarm
clock would wake me up, whirring, at six.
Then I had to wake my charges—no light
task. I would go down to the kitchen and
make their breakfast, come back with it, and
then start to dress and wash the children
with all the usual palaver---for one of them

wouldn't want to be washed, the other would put his breeches on wrong way round, and the third refuse to take his milk. In fact I had to cope with all their childish misdemeanours, and the job was by no means a sinecure, as I have already said. At length, towards 7.30, Grock the nursery-maid would be seen leaving the house with all three rascals, the eldest in front, the other two holding on to my hands in the rear. Once I had taken them to school I was due in the workshop. I would call for them again at midday, and in the afternoon would instruct them in French and wash them and put them to bed in the evening. I used to love taking them to the synagogue of a Saturday, and was never tired of listening to the Elder's mournful chanting.

This episode in my life seemed to go on endlessly till one day I found myself selling violin strings to a member of a well known musical quartette. He suddenly asked me:

"Do you know anyone who plays the fiddle?"

"Yes. I do. I also play the xylophone and mandolin."

"Excellent! Come to the Kronengarten this evening!"

I put the children early to bed, and myself pretended to drop off to sleep, for the Sternberg household was run on strict lines. Towards ten o'clock I crept out of the house, reported at the Kronengarten, and made the acquaintance of my new associates, with whom I played till four in the morning. But when I had repeated this escapade three times Sternberg found me out! He was not at all the sort to overlook it. I must either look after the children or fiddle. One or the other! The decision was easy. I was consequently cashiered from my office of nursemaid. And, so with a blessed sense of newly-won freedom, I threw in my lot with the merry musicians.

18

THE FIRE EATER AND HIS WIFE

AND now began a life for me that really seems hardly credible when I look back, for sheer, utter confusion. It is all I can do to disentangle names, dates and happenings. Everything seems one bewildering jumble of want and superfluity, love, hate and sympathy, and I just stand beneath it and let it gush down on me like a waterfall.

A few days after my first appearance in the Kronengarten, where I had been playing both fiddle and xylophone, as well as clowning, a quiet and thoughtful looking man came to see me, who was also a clown, looking for a partner. He told me his name, Massimo Spitz. It was a name I knew and liked the sound of.

"You'll take it on?"

"Rather!"

"Yes—but at once? I've got all the instruments and costumes. You needn't find a thing."

I gave such an inward leap for joy that my heart nearly collided with my Adam's apple. "Who knows, perhaps this is the great beginning!" I wrote a perfectly beautiful farewell letter to the Schrammel Quartette, and next morning we set off, third-class, to Grosswardein. We rehearsed in the train, a dress rehearsal, complete with comic clothes and paint, as well as fiddle, drum and xylophone, and the peasants travelling with us nearly died of laughter. They positively made us get out at every station and drink with them, promising us pyramids of baked meats and oceans of Tokay, would we but go to see them in their villages. All the railway employees drank with us—engine driver, station officials, and of course the passengers.

So elated was the whole personnel that the train forgot to go on, and we departed, hell for leather, an hour late. The tipsy engine driver invited us to sit next him on the engine. The rascal took his bends at such a rate we were within an ace of going off the rails and being killed to a man! As for me, I was so elated I crept on to the steam whistle when the train was going at its maddest speed and sat myself firmly down. And that

is how we finally arrived at our destination
with a clown on top of the engine. All Grosswardein hummed with it and it served as the
most admirable advertisement; the very first
evening our open-air arena was crowded out,
and so it was to the end of our stay.

Then, back once more to Budapest.
Here we were joined by Piselli, a congenial
and high-spirited colleague, and together we
appeared as the Massimo Troupe for two
months on end in the famous Ratay Circus.
By that time it was November, snow was falling already in the mountains, and circus
managers were rolling up their tents and
settling down to their winter sleep.

All the same, we had got to live. In a
certain café we were accosted by a handsome,
well-formed man who came up to our table.
He was Purischkewitsch, the trick-rider—
every inch of him a trick-rider, I can assure
you. He suggested to us a winter tour through
villages and small towns. We were only too
delighted. The troupe was formed then and
there and consisted of Purischkewitsch, Piselli, Spitz and myself, together with Fracassa, a fire-eater and Adelaide, the tight-
rope walker.

Adelaide and Fracassa were husband and wife. He was a fire-eater just such as you see in the picture-books, with singed eyelashes and eyebrows, red-rimmed eyes and a tawny, bulbous nose, that looked half burned. His mouth was as wide as an oven door, and his teeth black from fire-eating. His voice was like the rasping of a knife on metal and he had a cauldron that might have been used for a prehistoric monster. Adelaide had coal-black hair and eyes to match that stabbed you through and through; her skin was snow-white, and she had a way of always showing her beautifully formed teeth. We all fell for her from the very first moment—I most of all. I flattered myself that I found most favour in her sight—such favours, oh, such very delectable favours! The fire-eater was terribly jealous and would spew out of his mouth all the fire he had been supposed to swallow, and rage like a demented steam-hammer.

Our tour did not begin particularly well in the little country town of Miskols. The fire-eater had made his fiery preparations too close to the wings during the show, with the result that the wings took fire, and a

143

panic ensued that I had much ado to calm down with laborious antics. We performed at six places on end after this fashion, with Fire-Eater, Tight-rope Dancer, Acrobat and music, and each of us earned, on an average, three gulden an evening.

One night our money-taker bolted with the till. I no longer remember the name of the small Carpathian town in which we were left stranded. Nothing attracts misfortune so much as misfortune. We were joined by four poor sons of the stage, typical strolling play-actors, and so starving and emaciated were they one was afraid to speak in their presence. We had a good hot meal served up to them and then agreed to join forces.

Our tour began. We included the actors with their sketch in the middle of our programme, and we comic artists provided the introduction and end. We went by sledge from place to place. The winter was cruelly severe, and wolves would howl in the forests around the little villages.

19

WE ARE ATTACKED BY WOLVES

THE jealousy of Fracassa was suddenly fanned to fever heat by a certain incident. A peasant had seen me kissing the tight-rope dancer behind a barn door, and the dirty dog had promptly gone and told on me. We were giving our show that evening, and according to the bill I came before the fire-eater. After my turn was over I hurried away, having appointed to meet Adelaide in her room during her husband's enforced absence on the stage. I go racing up the stairs, burst open the door, enter with arms outspread— and there before me stands the fire-eater, stick in hand and red as a beet with rage. I stand, staring at the giant's open mouth. I don't know to this day how it was he was able to forestall me. He snarled out:

"What do you want?"

"I ... I only wanted to say good evening to your wife ..."

"Look here, young lad ... if you value the

bones in your body, you'll give up this habit of saying good evening..."

On which he held up his cudgel on high like the bough of a tree. I dodged for all I was worth.

Some days later we were playing in a neighbouring village. I shall never forget the night that followed that show. We had found a lodging place with some Jews in the village. In one corner of the horrible, close little room slept Adelaide and her fire-eater, while in the bed against the opposite wall slumbered Spitz and myself. Slumbered, forsooth! The only one to sleep was the fire-eater, and he lay with his face to the wall, snoring fit to wake the dead. None of the rest of us slept a wink, but it wasn't only the snoring kept us awake.

Adelaide lay next to her snoring beetroot. I couldn't see her face as the corner her bed was in was so dark, but in the half-light I could detect her hand, softly moving, as though making signs to mine. On which I stretched out my hand, but they were not near enough to meet. Spitz by my side was tossing and turning and biting his pillows in the throes of desire. Through the little window a glimpse could be caught of the starry night, while outside, in the forest, the wolves kept howling.

This situation was unbearable. I suddenly got up, slipped on my shoes and coat, and went out into the snowy, December night. The church clock struck two. Damn the woman . . . damn her . . . damn her . . . damn her . . . I stamped my way down the snow-strewn village street, and had soon left the last houses behind me. The street merged into the plain in front of the great forest. The sky was full of stars and fleecy cloudlets. A stone's throw from where I stood was a little hill.

All at once I saw a constellation I had never noticed in my life before. It must have risen above the horizon and was now on a level with the hill. I had never pretended to know much about the stars, but like most other folk, I could recognise the principal constellations—the Great Bear and Orion, and so forth. But never before had I seen six stars all in a row, six stars of a fiery red . . . never before, to my knowledge. And now, all of a sudden, if two of the stars didn't start to move away with the most rapid, discon-

certing movements, while directly afterwards
the rest started to do the same thing. In fact,
the entire constellation seemed rushing at me
in utmost confusion down the hill! And now
I knew what those stars were and that they
were stars on four legs!

I tore up that village street for dear life,
for already I could hear the brutes behind
me, panting and yammering. At the last
moment I sprang through the sheltering door
and bolted it behind me. Never again . . .
Never again . . .!

The next day we ordered sledges to take us
a three hours' journey to the next village
where we were due The sledges were ready
for us towards twilight. The snow had ceased
to fall. Wood-cutters came and told us the
best route through the forest so as to avoid
the larger snowdrifts. We must start then
and there if we wanted to arrive in time. It
was four already. The journey would take
us three hours, and then we should have one
hour left for unpacking, making up and
getting into our clothes. As a matter of fact,
I was under-dressed in my tights already.

The peasants seemed to think we would do
better to stay one more night where we were

149

and go on the next day. From the sound of the trees in the forest and the direction of the wind, coming from the West, they predicted another snow-storm. The villagers pointed up to the sky, saying "Storm . . . Storm . . ." though they really meant something quite different. For that matter, each one of us was thinking of a certain peril we would not so much as breathe to one another, from fear of demoralising what little courage we had left for the drive.

We got into the sledges that were provided with thick, warm furs. Rifles were distributed among us, one to each sledge. Adelaide had wangled it so that I sat next to her. The fire-eater had concealed an enormous brandy flask in the front sledge. For the last time the peasants shook us by the hand, the driver clicked with his tongue, and off we went, westwards. Before us stretched the murky forest, and overhead the sky was full of thick snow-clouds. I snuggled up to Adelaide like anything. The storm was less heavy than we had expected. Very little fresh snow fell, and though the tree tops continued to rustle, we drove through a silent world, our sledges gliding along the snowy ground without a

Photo. Dephot

"I'M A-COMING. . . . I'M A-COMING. . . ."

Photo. Stone, Berlin

" . . . . THAT I'M ONE OF THE BEST CONCERTINA PLAYERS!"

sound, save for the puffing of the horses. Already we calculated to have done half the distance. An hour and a half left to us—let us make the most of it! And so we lay in one another's arms, swimming, as the poets have it, in a sea of bliss! Utter darkness wrapped us around, we couldn't even any more see the driver sitting in front of us, or even one another. We only felt each the other's presence. But suddenly the sledge gave a bound forward, and our heads knocked together so that a sea of sparks flew before my eyes.

The horses had suddenly increased their pace, changing their trot into a sharp gallop. The driver succeeded in calming them, but I knew, from what the peasants had told me, how infallibly horses can scent danger . . . I strained every muscle of my ears; no microphone, I am sure, could have been more susceptible to sound than I was at that moment, but I heard nothing but the crunching of our runners on the snowy track, and the regular beat of the horses' hooves.

Through a gap in the forest we caught sight of distant lights twinkling through a mist. Once again immersed in the darkness of the fir trees, I remembered seeing mys-

L

terious lights when crossing the fields that separated the forests—they must surely be the lights of distant villages that according to the peasants' description lay about an hour's distance from our goal. We had still three-quarters of an hour to go. Make hay while the sun shone! I buried my head in Adelaide's arm and continued to doze.

I was awakened by a still more violent jolt. The horses had turned the sledge sheer round and were off at a gallop. So excited were they that the driver could no longer calm them and it was all he could do to hold them in. Their hooves pelted us with snow. Adelaide clung tight to me. The horses' neighing sounded like a lamentation! We were sprinkled with froth now.

We were going back on our tracks . . . back into the forest! Those sparks, surely, proceeded from my own eyes only! That was it, of course . . . my very own eyes! I rubbed my lids . . . But there were the sparks, still all around us, as though rising from some secret, hidden conflagration!

The gleaming eyes of the wolves now united in wedge-shaped formation, moving against us. The slow members of the pack were at the base of it, the quick ones at the peak. More and more the wedge tapered to a point. Six pair of eyes . . . then five . . . then four . . . then three . . . while the distance betwixt pursuers and pursued grew smaller and smaller In the phosphorescent gleam that enwrapped them I could already detect the steaming breath of the furthermost brute. Two pairs of eyes! And now for a good straight aim between those two fiery sparks, and *peng!* A sound of howling, and the sparks go out . . . *peng* . . . and *peng* again . . . and still more howling—terrible shrill screams. And now something really remarkable happens. In a trice, all the sparks go out, quite suddenly, and in their place arises a snarling and growling as though the whole pack were bent on nothing less than self murder. Which is precisely what has happened. The brutes have abandoned us and in their own beastly way are fighting over their dead comrades and who shall eat them. That gives us our chance! On we tear—to safety!

An hour later we were sitting in the village inn with steaming bowls of hot food in front of us and full bottles. The show must go to pot. In its place our friends the peasants entertained us, right royally. I had to relate my heroic exploit again and again. Adelaide's lover's glances did much to stimulate my imagination. My soul was at fever heat with love, wine and heroic impulses, and when morning broke I was drinking eternal brotherhood with the fire-eater.

This same brotherhood and mutual goodwill lasted precisely one day, after which the fiend—that arch-fiend, Woman—broke loose once more. Adelaide had played fast and loose with us all. She had raised the hopes of every one of us, letting the drawbridge down, so to say, before our expectant eyes, but the moment we any of us tried to cross the bridge—hey presto! she was off and away, and bestowing her favours on another. In inarticulate wrath we strutted around one another like so many jealous roosters with comb on end. Our shows became more and more indifferent, all our enthusiasm for them having ebbed away, our wardrobe quite frequently would get left behind, and we would play in freezing rooms for the simple reason that none of us had remembered to heat them. Each played only so as to give offence to the other whenever possible. Our audiences got smaller and smaller and finally ceased to exist.

One morning the sledges stood, as usual, ready to take us away. Fracassa and Adelaide took their places in the first sledge, and then ensued the usual jostle and scramble for the third seat by Adelaide's side. Suddenly all our long suppressed venom broke out on every side, and then began a pretty chemozzle! Everybody smote everybody else, and if possible took him by the throat, flung him down and stamped on him. Round where we fought the snow was cleared as though a steam plough had been at work! In the midst of all our oaths and curses might be heard the shrill and scornful laughter of the woman for whose sake we were tearing one another to pieces; the sound of it caused us to set to with redoubled ardour. When we finally desisted from sheer exhaustion, standing there with bleeding noses, regarding our battle in all its glory of white and red, the true Swiss colours . . .

Hallo . . . Hallo . . .

We rubbed our eyes. Had we drubbed one another blind? Adelaide and the fire-eater had vanished, together with the sledge! Not a trace of them! They had slipped away unnoticed.

In my first impulse of despair I jumped on one of the other sledges to pursue the fugitives, but my pals seized the horses by the bridle and dragged me from my seat.

"Let them go, man . . . let them go . . ."

We let them go and I have never seen or heard of either of them from that day to this. It was high time it happened. The very next day we felt as though a load had slipped from our shoulders, and were the best of friends, as is always the case when men are left to themselves and not plagued by women.

The snow now fell so heavily as to be almost uncanny. The wolves were so hungry that the peasants were forced to organise hunts against them. After a specially hard winter, skeletons of lonely wanderers are always unearthed in a forest in spring time— the wolves' victims. When this particular winter had passed, with its cruel frost, they are said to have found in the forest, at quite a short distance from the roadway, human bones and the bones of horses, lying around a dilapidated sledge.

20

ANOTHER SURPRISE

ALTHOUGH our company was now short of two, we made up for it by better and more conscientious work, and for the first time for many a day we began to collect good audiences and make good money. Not one word was ever again said about Adelaide.

But this improvement on our part lasted but one little week, at the end of which time we were as slack and casual as ever. I think our various temperaments were, from the beginning, ill suited to one another. We played to empty halls and the landlords finally refused to let out their rooms to us. For very hunger and cold we would often lie all day long in our wooden cubicles, aimlessly lying about and waiting—what for?

One morning, after a perishing and sleepless night I was rummaging aimlessly about in my box and came across the tuning set given to me by Sternberg. Holy smoke, here was an idea! I promptly asked the lodging-

house keeper who possessed a piano in this
village. He said the parson did. Whereupon
I donned a clean shirt, put on my best tie and
called at his house.

"Certainly... certainly... my piano hasn't
been tuned for the past seven years! How
much would you charge to do it?"

"Ten gulden."

"Isn't that rather a lot?"

"Oh, but, sir—seven years! Most pianos
are tuned twice a year, at a customary charge
of four gulden a time. So, if you'll just reckon
it up . . . seven times twice four . . . that
makes 56 . . . so in the ordinary way you
would have had to pay 56 gulden for piano-
tuning in those seven years . . . Instead of
which I am only asking ten for the whole
caboodle . . ."

The good man allowed himself to be persuaded, not only paying me the ten gulden
but recommending me to a certain Count
who had a house in the neighbourhood.

These pianos could only be suffering from
a mortal disease of the bones. The count's
piano certainly was. No sooner did I touch
the keys than the hammers tinkled as if
against glass. Clouds of yellow dust emerged

from every rent and cranny, and a whole horde of moths flew into the light so soon as I had opened the lid of the sounding board. The moths had eaten away all the felting of the hammers, and the wood of the hammers themselves was so rotten it simply fell to pieces when touched. I cut fresh hammers from bits of oak, and renewed the felting from an old Borsalino hat that the Count willingly sacrificed. At the end of a week I was able to coax a melody out the resuscitated piano: it was not, I admit, the "Rain Prelude," but the Radetzky march with which the Count was duly impressed and delighted.

He in his turn recommended me to a friend, and *he* to a Countess: the Countess passed me on to another parson, who sent me to a Baroness and the Baroness to a Baron, and so for the space of a week I trudged from parsonage to castle and country residence, resurrecting a dozen dead and antiquated pianos, and inspiring their ghostly strings to fresh harmonies. It was work that brought me in touch with strange places and still stranger people, both infinitely remote from the world of modern life. These castles and country estates in the heart of the great, wintry forest were more like mausoleums than the habitations of live people, and those who lived in them often looked as though they had been dead already, months on end and buried into the bargain.

There came an evening in one particularly desolate place when I had need of all my Swiss cool-headedness not to rush out into the night, anywhere—to the wolves in the forest, if need be rather than stay in this abode that resembled nothing so much as the grimmest kind of fairy story. The castle was plump in the middle of the wood; it was furnished, in the approved fashion, with drawbridge and moat, and towers built in by jackdaws. The window of the music room, wherein stood an attenuated mahogany piano, looked on to a dark and snowy forest ravine. A certain Countess N——, divorced from her husband, inhabited this castle, together with a butler, a couple of servants and a moth-eaten poodle. This aged dame was an incurable coquette who had already sent many pathetically significant glances in my direction.

The piano was the happy hunting ground

and nursery of many mice. When testing some of the bass notes, the hammer must have struck a mouse's nest; no bass note was forthcoming, only some pitiful piping and squeaking, and no sooner had I raised the piano lid than a multitude of tails darted hither and thither seeking refuge; the same sort of situation, in fact, as when, many years later, I extracted a pair of corsets from the sound board in my famous turn with Anto-net. This gave me the idea for it.

After repeated efforts I had restored the piano to some sort of order, and cleaned it up. It was now late in the evening and snow was falling thickly and had been for some time; I was invited to stay till the following morning and offered a bed for the night.

The butler showed me up to my room. Then the Countess sent word to me that she would like me to take tea with her in her private apartment. An old servant conducted me up curving flights of Renaissance stairs, thence along dusky passages, hung with trophies of the chase, to a room decorated in the Arabian fashion—an exotic little room, reeking with perfume, lit with a rosy light from a praying lamp. Here awaited me the aged Countess, lying on a welter of cushions and dressed like a film adventuress.

Her artfully dyed black hair had a greenish shimmer, and locks of it fell over her eyes that shone with the gleam of bella donna. The wrinkles of that withered face were thickly painted out. The scraggy neck muscles were concealed by lace, though not too successfully. The garish red lips were pursed into an ingratiating smile, through which gleamed the gold-stopped teeth. With as good a grace as I could muster I kissed the ring-bestudded bony hand and took a seat. Joseph was never more embarrassed in the presence of Potiphar.

"Come and sit nearer to me, my young friend," chirped the old scarecrow. I obeyed. She poured out the tea, pressed pralines upon me and cigarettes. I lit a cigarette and toyed in the utmost confusion with a chocolate biscuit, gulping down my tea without being able to utter one word. I could only feel the devouring looks she cast at me.

"My *dear*," . . . she suddenly whispered . . . and I could sense a warm, moist fin feeling for my hand. In utter consternation I let her get hold of it and caress it.

GROCK

"Tell me now . . . tell me now . . . dear boy . . . I am still desirable—isn't it so?" she wheezed at me, throwing back her silken negligée and revealing herself with nothing on underneath—nothing, that is, but a bag of skin and bones. With one bound I was at the door, but Circe leaped after me, and encircled me so tight with her spider's limbs that for a moment there seemed no way of escape. With the strength of despair I wrenched the hands asunder that she was clasping round my neck, shook her off, opened the door and fled. Fled, helter-skelter, through passages, down stairs and then along an open gallery that ran alongside the snowy forest ravine. I had had my belly full. Paul de Kock himself had never conjured up anything more macabre!

I worked my way through a series of stairs, passages and galleries, till I found myself outside by the front door. I rang the bell. The butler answered it, and with a face of infinite astonishment showed me up to my room once more. Very early next morning I drove back to the little country town—a journey of some three hours—where my friends awaited me. I charged up a bill of forty gulden to the

Countess, ten hours at four gulden an hour.
I got it, too. Cheap at the price, for such an
evening.

21

AN INFERNAL MACHINE

Heigh-ho for Hungary again!

With the money I had earned by tuning pianos, nearly a thousand gulden, I was able to take a decisive step; I bought railway tickets for our four play-actors to Budapest, pressing upon them twenty-five gulden apiece for expenses, saw them to the station, said a cordial farewell to them and waved them off. Then, together with Spitz, I went up to Temesvar, where we played before a thousand spectators and worked the same night at the Casino, before the officers of the local garrison. We had enough now for the Balkan tour we so much wanted to do. We put in a fortnight at Belgrade at the "Concert du Boulevard." My memories of Belgrade consist of down-at-heel soldiers, pavements, crazy and cracked as a Rhone glacier, and a perpetual stink of mutton fat. Every day, in the *pension* we stayed at, we had served up to us, morning and evening, mutton

READY TO GO ON!

MY WARDROBE

stew with potatoes, two weeks on end. Mutton stew . . . mutton stew . . . mutton stew . . . we positively reeked like sheep ourselves at the end of it.

One morning I caught sight of the cook, an enormous and dirty woman, buying potatoes in the market. From what particular knacker's stall would she purchase our meat, I wondered. I followed her, unnoticed, into a side street. There she disappeared into some underground cellar that was full of sheep's meat, skinned and dried. She bought a portion of this mummied flesh and shook it so that white clouds of maggots came out on every side. Then this female abortion took the joint of mutton in one hand and her great potato basket in the other, and went on her homeward way like the Megæra she was. Mutton stew, since then, has never been my favourite dish.

This same day, by the grace of God, our Belgrade date came to an end. We took the train for Sofia that night. The Orient Express proving too dear for us, we must needs travel by a common or garden train that in those days used to trundle, for the benefit of the common herd, between Belgrade and Con-

M

stantinople, stopping at nearly every station and picking up numberless specimens on its way of the dregs of humanity from the Further East. The passengers were a mixed crew of shoddy agents, bullies, prostitutes, robbers, thieves, crooks, sharpers and revolutionaries—none of them missing! They clotted together in a congealed mass, snoring, kissing, screeching and cursing in chorus. I need not add that all the windows were tight closed and that the habits of this crew were more than revolting. The cooking establishment was stowed away behind the engine. The cook would stagger along with a couple of steaming cauldrons, and each passenger would have his portion of food ladled out into tin plates and cups. One of the cauldrons contained—need I say it?—mutton stew, and the other coffee. I believe the coffee was made of mutton, too; it had a muttony and pestilential smell.

We got out at Sofia, feeling contaminated inside and out, and took good care to air ourselves for the space of a whole day outside the town before we once again dared mix with our fellow creatures. When we finally turned up at the music-hall it was only to find that

the manager had gone bankrupt. The French
Consul assisted us out of our difficulties in
the most obliging fashion, and even helped
organise an entertainment that we gave in
the Consulate.

I now went on alone, my goal being Constantinople. My dream was, if possible, to
give a show before no less a person than the
Sultan of Turkey! French colleagues had
told me marvellous yarns of the famous
despot's whimsical turn of mind. When
Sarah Bernhardt was in Constantinople,
Abdul Hamid had invited her to give a performance in his private theatre. He himself
attended it, together with his entire harem.
These three hundred favoured ladies sat in
boxes behind golden bars, and chattered. The
great Panjandrum sat in solitary state in the
Sultan's box in the middle of the theatre.
When the play was over, up got the Khalif,
and with his own hands skilfully threw a red
silk purse of jingling coin on to the stage.
That purse contained a thousand Turkish
pounds—in other words, twenty-three thousand francs! That, at any rate, is the story.

I already saw myself appointed Mahomm-
medan Court Jester. Why not? Abdul Hamid

was reported to have a weakness for Swiss. My thoughts turned to the career of Gottfried Stucki, a countryman of mine whom I knew slightly. He would be the first person for me to look up in Constantinople. Stucki had formerly been head waiter in the best hotel in Constantinople, till one day his boss sent him over to the *selamlik* on the occasion of the weekly reception given by the Sultan to the foreign diplomats. Stucki was to deputise for the official Wine Pourer (gone sick) whose office it was to dispense champagne in the approved fashion to the assembled guests. The very next day the lucky card was appointed to a special post of Arch Champagne Pourer, receiving from the Sultan a monthly salary of one hundred pounds (2,300 francs). He was to be in residence at the *selamlik* and be known henceforth as Stucki Bey!

Dallying with visions such as this, I was swept over the Bulgarian cornfields on my way to Adrianople, the first great Turkish city. Arriving there meant customs and luggage inspection. My passport was pronounced in order, but the official made a frightful fuss on going through my luggage. Amongst my

goods and chattels he had discovered a patent
contraption for making fizzy lemonade, much
in use in those days, part of the outfit being
small cartridges of carbonic acid that were
packed separately from the wicker-covered
flask. These tubby little things certainly had
all the appearance of ammunition.

It was an infernal machine! In a trice I
was surrounded by a dozen policemen and
officials, who seized me by the scruff of the
neck and searched me to my very in'nards.
The "bombs" were passed from hand to hand
with the utmost caution and examined. I
was subjected to an exhaustive examination.
Heaven knows where I hadn't come from!
In vain did I try to prove to them my native
Swiss innocuousness, in vain did I offer to
demonstrate the harmlessness of my lemonade syphon by a practical exhibition, in vain
—my last trump of all—did I call on the
name of my eminent countryman Stucki
Bey. "To hell with Stucki Bey" . . . that was
all they answered. Or the equivalent for it,
in Turkish.

At last the bandy-legged old *Pasha*—I
observed they all addressed him as Pasha
Effendi—allowed me to try the perilous ex-

periment. The police stood expectantly around me in a circle, I poured water into the flask, added a little sugar and some lemon juice, placed the cartridge upon the hole, pressed with the iron ramrod—the thing fizzed and the lemonade was ready. On which I uncorked the flask, filled a glass with lemonade and everyone tasted it in turn. They began to smile, all of them. The Pasha begged my pardon, but did not give me permission to proceed with my journey.

The World War arose from a dispute about the Turkish heir. The ancient Kingdom of Turkey had become degenerate from the fault of a gloomy, neurotic, timorous, enervated ruler. I would have made even Abdul Hamid laugh. He might have kept me in his service. Who knows if the history of the world would not thereby have been altered?

I returned to Budapest where I again joined up with Spitz. The next people to employ us were a man and his wife from Bohemia, who owned a circus. Ratay, the husband, was a kindly person, and his colossal spouse, who always sat at the receipt of custom, had a heart of gold.

It was spring, and again we started off on

tour through villages and towns, the whole
troupe of us parading through all the streets,
on horseback, publicly before each show, preceded by four trumpeters. Then we came up
against Leo's Travelling Circus. This circus
contained a potent attraction for Spitz, for
working in it as a trick-rider was Charlotte,
to whom he was secretly betrothed. But
Charlotte's stepfather, Wilson, who used to
be in the *gendarmerie* and was now a heavy-
weight athlete, also in the service of Leo,
hated Spitz, and the couple could only indulge in stolen meetings.

Leo ended by engaging us, and then the inevitable situation arose. Wilson, rehearsing
in the arena with his wife, a hefty athlete,
saw us come in, stopped working and made at
us with curses. What right had the rogue
got to attack me like that, an utter stranger,
and nothing in the least to do with him? My
blood rose, and I landed him "one on the
boko" that laid him out flat. His substantial better half, seeing how things were, discarded her iron rings, and with two well
placed blows promptly made me measure my
length on the ground. It was all in the day's
work for a woman like that. I scrambled to

my feet, while Wilson did the same, and rushed towards me with clenched fists, but I held him off by blowing at him, and as I was already bleeding from both nose and mouth he recoiled from the nasty mess I was, and actually began to roar with laughter at the comic aspect of it all. On which we all joined in. We became excellent friends, and Spitz won his Charlotte.

One morning the brokers called on Leo and removed everything he had—tent, instruments and horses. But one door shuts and another opens. We took an engagement, at a mere pittance, with the Moses Circus, a potty little concern that was really simply a family affair, consisting of Father Moses, Mother Moses and six little Moseses. All of them, old as well as young, went barefoot and bare-headed, and their little tent was so torn and patched together it could hardly hold. None the less we went into Tokay for the great yearly market! That was to be my last appearance in Hungary for many years. We used to start work at six in the morning and never leave off before one at night; it was strenuous but very good. For a whole week on end the peasants kept us drunk with the wine they treated us to, and we played and anticked like so many gods.

To my sorrow, the morning we were due to leave, I overheard Charlotte whispering to her Spitz in the next cubby-hole: "Directly we get the chance, we'll get rid of Adrien; we don't really need him, now . . ."

That was enough for me; I packed up my bundle and vanished without leave-taking. An hour later I was in the train to Budapest. I arrived there as yellow as a lemon, having contracted jaundice on the way. For a week I dragged myself miserably about, bitter at heart till one morning I ran into the Barogoldi Circus in a small forest town. A clown I knew recognised me; stooped down and spat in my face by way of greeting. I adopted a sparring attitude.

"Put up, you fool—you'll be all right in three days!"

And as a matter of fact I was. The shock of surprise had driven away my jaundice.

22

THE SWISS NATIONAL CIRCUS

I THINK I like Spaniards and Hungarians best of all nationalities. Both are people of strong and magnanimous impulses . . . they are so romantic, so "unmodern," so readily accessible. My life in Hungary was really only a preparation for my life in Spain. That is where I first came into my own.

I had a moderately good time before that, in France. It began with something of a stir at a Lyons circus. During the third week of an engagement there, in the middle of the show my partner, a rather difficult and conceited sort of chap, suddenly sat himself down in a chair, not in the least according to programme, and addressed me in stentorian and authoritative tones, stroking an imaginary moustache, the while, military fashion:

"Get me on to the President of the Republic . . . at once!"

The audience roared. But I could see in a jiffy that this was no play acting; the fellow was in dead earnest, his face was crimson and his eyes gleaming. He now drew himself up in the most majestic fashion, turned round slowly, lifted his coat tails, waggled his behind at me and commanded:

"Kiss me, minion" . . .

The audience was convulsed. He started to bellow:

"Hold your tongues, all of you! Stand up everyone . . . Don't you dare to speak . . . Stand to attention . . . Don't you know whose presence you're in? I am Kaiser Wilhelm!"

On which the house was beside itself. The man had gone suddenly and completely mad, and was removed then and there to an asylum, a diplomatic crisis thereby being nipped in the bud.

Two colleagues of mine the Brothers Barasetta, with whom I got on admirably, suggested we clubbed together and founded a circus. "We've got the stuff; a stage and a trapeze and five tent poles. No tent, though, unfortunately. Still—what do we want with a tent? These lovely summer nights we can play in the open air!" Right-oh!

Our stuff was ready and waiting for us at Voiron, a little town not far from Lyons. It was early evening when we got there. The five tent poles had already been put up in the big, deserted market-place, and on the little stage two magnificent women were sitting and waiting for us—Spaniards, with sombre and sensitive faces; next them sat an emaciated acrobat. These Spaniards were the mother and sister of my colleague. They rose without a word as we came up. There they stood, wrapped around in their long, dark cloaks, with the silver spangles of their acrobats' costumes glimmering beneath. I was terribly impressed with their distinguished appearance, and made my best bow: it was a curious introduction, with almost a note of solemnity in it.

The show that we started with an hour later attracted but few spectators, and neither of the ladies, in consequence, made an appearance. All the same, the audience had something for their money. It was the little acrobat who, for the most part, had to make up for the curtailed programme.

Never had any artist made such an impression upon me. The trapeze was strung between two of the poles, on a rope of about twelve metres long. Thomas—for that was his name—clambered up the rope ladder, unhitched the trapeze from the pole to which it was fastened, and swung out on it into space. And space it really was, for it was like swinging out over the Alps into Lombardy! The Square was barely lit save for the brightly shining stars. Seen from below, Thomas looked to be flashing through the skies, freed from all earthly control.

"There he is . . . there he is . . . no, there he is . . .!" the audience sat whispering. This bold night-flyer really had to be sought for in the clouds, so mighty were the bounds he described, and when you looked for him in the east, there he was in exactly the opposite direction, amid the western stars. This great artist, Thomas, is now seventy years old and working yet. I hear he is fresh as a boy still, and prospers well.

We say goodbye. I am suddenly weary of my tramping life. The proprietor of a café in Voiron had offered me the job of pianist at ten francs a day, free board and lodging, and I had accepted.

This new life had lasted exactly ten days when one morning the entire town was posted with bills announcing the arrival of the "Swiss National Circus." It had come in over night, and the great tent was already set up in the Square. I was sitting practising the piano in the café when two ladies came in, one elderly, the other young and beautiful. They were trying to find a room for the duration of the circus season. That they were circus folk I knew at a glance. Suddenly, the younger smiled at me:

"Why, we know one another! Aren't you Adrian Wettach?"

"Why . . . it's Marie . . . no . . . wait a moment . . . it's Jenny Wetzel!"

And so it was! Jenny, the daughter of my father's crony, the little star of the Col des Roches Troupe and Carnival nights at Bienne —the admiration of my boyhood days! I had never seen her since. She was married now to a Frenchman named Lucien Godard and both were engaged with the National Circus . . . I lost no time in accompanying Jenny into the Square, where she introduced me to Godard. We shook hands like old friends.

"Why don't you come along with us?" Godard suggested.

"Yes . . . do come . . ." from Jenny.

"Of course he'll come," somebody behind us wheezed.

I turned round and beheld a little fat, beaming creature with a rosy countenance.

"A true Swiss at last! I'd recognise the Jura note, anywhere! Welcome . . . welcome . . . good countryman! My name is Schmidt . . . Schmidt . . ."

He held out his reddened hands to me that I seized and shook heartily. A quarter of an hour later I was engaged as Circus Cashier for two hundred and fifty francs!

Papa Schmidt had a very special feeling for Swiss. Of the forty members of his National Circus, only the Proprietor, his wife, and the bill-sticker were of genuine Swiss origin, and the patriotic little man regarded this circumstance as almost a form of treachery. My engagement, therefore, was preceded by an interrogation as searching as it was concise.

"Come along, come along," ordered Schmidt, almost forcibly extracting me from my friends. He could scarcely wait till I was sitting opposite him in the caravan. He now slid his horn-rimmed spectacles on to the tip of his fat nose, and blinked at me above the glasses, interrogative fashion:

"You've been to school?"

"Certainly, Herr Schmidt."

"Christened and confirmed?"

"Certainly, Herr Schmidt."

"Not Catholic, I *hope?*"

"Evangelical . . ."

"I *thought* so . . ."

"Why?"

"There's Catholic noses and there's Evangelical noses. Yours is Evangelical, and all the better for it."

"Oh . . . surely not?"

"Tell me now—what's the Capital of Switzerland?"

"Berne."

"Good. Tell me the names of some Swiss heroes."

"Tell . . . Winkelried . . ."

I stopped in my efforts not to burst out laughing in the face of this enchanting character. On which he became impatient.

"Get on . . . get on . . ."

"Waldmann . . ."

Again I dried up. On which he burst out, infinitely peeved:

"And Ochsenbein?   Never heard of Ochsenbein?"

"Lord save us . . . who *was* Ochsenbein?"

WAIT, MY LAD!

HOW MUCH?

"Mean to say you've never heard of *Och-senbein* . . . that great fighting rebel . . . A pretty countryman you are!"

The connection was made clear to me later. Schmidt came from Lucerne, and Lucerne was the headquarters of the "Son-derbund," or League of the Roman Catholic Cantons of Switzerland. Schmidt, being an ardent opponent of the Pope, had infinite enthusiasm for Ochsenbein, head of the anti-Catholic movement.

Vater Schmidt was quite the most lovable and original employer I ever had. He had taken to the circus from the butchering trade. For thirty years he had been slaughtering cattle and chopping up meat, scraping and scrimping all the time with a view to purchas-ing a travelling circus. For a butcher to transform himself into a Circus Director means exchanging the safest of all trades for the most uncertain. There's an example for you! I recommend it to the notice of all those profiteers and get-rich-quick gentlemen whose one idea is to feather their nest and then lie back and wallow in it for the rest of their days!

23

SPAGHETTI

I took the money and cleaned out the ring
... I was cashier and stable-boy rolled into
one ... I kept the books ... I did the shop-
ping ... I groomed the horses ... I cleaned
the harness ... I mended the tent, and for the
big pole I cut out a colossal Swiss flag that
proved to be so heavy that no east or west
wind had strength enough to flap it! Nothing
but the "Föhn," that thaw-wind that storms
down its crazy way from the Alps, could
move it. That did the business, and Papa
Schmidt was so delighted he made me climb
up a hill with him outside the town, whence
we could look down upon the valley. The
majestic Swiss standard flying from the
circus tent certainly was a goodly sight to behold, in this warm, southern valley.

On we went from town to town up the
valley of the Rhone, skirting the Paradise of
Provence, where the good God surely passes
all his spring holidays; we touched Avignon,

Arles, Tarascon, and the Swiss National Circus actually set itself up in the great Roman arena of Nîmes! Could there have been a fitter place?

One morning, Vater Schmidt exhorted me to leave the pay-box and once again perform in the Ring. It was a family affair. His son-in-law wanted to sit at the receipt of custom!

"Wettach, you oughtn't to be hiding that light of yours under a bushel! You owe it to yourself and your native land . . ."

The exhortation was as unnecessary as it was irresistible. Twice within the past six months I had had the till I was in charge of broken into and robbed. To the tune of five hundred francs, compensation money! I had had more than enough of the managerial side.

Now for my partner! There was a certain couple of comics, Brick and Brock, to whom I was given a strong recommendation by a colleague. They had been obliged to separate owing to the exigencies of military service, and Brick had now just served his time. I wrote to him at Marseilles, and the result was the appearance of Marius Galante, alias Brick in person. We liked one another. He was a splendid, intelligent fellow. We soon got out a scheme of action, and after rehearsing together all one day, we made our appearance in the Swiss National Circus.

"Brick and Wettach . . . sounds rotten . . ." I declared.

"What d'you suggest?"

"Well, your other partner was Brock. From now on I'll call myself Grock. Brick and Grock . . ."

That's how the name Grock happened. I made my first bow as Grock in the arena at Nîmes in a skit on Papa Schmidt, with a huge false stomach and a devastating tendency to asthma that kept on getting the better of me and at length completely prostrated me, to the great delight of the spectators. And no one laughed more loudly than the subject of our parody.

Brick in his best days was bad to beat. I got an unforgettable amount from him, those three years we worked together. He and I trapsed about through the goodly land of France, on tour for many a day. At length I saw Paris. Actually the dream of my youth came true, and I was playing in the Cirque Medrano! We also played in Belgium and in Spain, then took boat to Tunis and from Tunis on to Naples, where we appeared in the Salone Margherita.

That was my first voyage by sea, and I shall never forget it. A woman with a coming-on disposition started making eyes at me. We "clicked," so to say, at afternoon tea on the promenade deck. It was a beautiful, mild day, with a cloudless sky and a moderate sea. I emerged from my cabin immaculate, after the most laborious toilet, clad in a white silk shirt and spotless suit of flannels. The lady was already waiting for me and smiling at a distance. My way went past the ship's bridge; and I could see the Captain also enjoying a little feminine recreation, leaning over the taffrail with an attractive Daughter of the South.

But just when I went peacocking along, the catastrophe happened. We passengers had indulged in a lunch that day that was certainly excellent in itself, but perhaps not wholly judicious for weak digestions, easily affected by the ship's motion. The menu consisted of *spaghetti alle vonghole* (spaghetti served with little shell fish dressed in oil), followed by chocolate cream, the whole washed down with Burgundy, *ad lib*. To my unutterable horror, I suddenly gave a loud hiccup, and before I could even turn away, I was festooned with the hideous garland of my spaghetti lunch . . . I will spare you further details . . . Suffice it to say that the tender attachment I had hoped to form did *not* stand the test. My hopes were for ever dashed. I never saw my charmer again, for the simple reason that I kept my cabin for the rest of the trip.

Our next journey by sea was as far as Buenos Aires. We sailed on the boat *Italia*. For eight whole days we had to lie in dock at St. Vincent, on the little island of Cape Verdi, for repairs to our rudder. The delay was well made up for by the friendly attitude of the nigger inhabitants. We gave these black friends of ours a free show one evening, just when the sun was sinking below the sea. The whole situation was most strange and unreal. Before us huddled a crowd of woolly-headed blacks, and in the background stretched a perfectly calm sea, with banks of rose-tinged cloud overhead. But the effect of our jokes was, not to make these light-hearted children of nature more light-hearted still, but to induce a profound melancholy; their broad faces grew more and more mournful; the corners of their mouths quivered, and presently the tears coursed down their cheeks. We had to abandon the entertainment.

I didn't see Buenos Aires again for another twenty years. I had my own reasons for not wanting to return. Never in all my life had Fate kept so many shocks in store for me up her sleeve as in that town. The very day after my arrival I sprained the ankle of my right foot, and had to spend a week in hospital. Three days later I slipped up on the tramway, and broke a bone in my leg: one month's hospital. Ten days after that, Brick slithered down the iron twirling staircase in the circus, on top of my head: my scalp was injured and I received a slight concussion: three weeks' hospital. And to crown all these misfortunes, Brick and I had a fisticuff set-to, tooth and nail, on account of a badly-tuned guitar.

"Why you can't keep your dirty paws off the darned thing beats me" . . . he snarled at me one evening, before the show.

"I tell you, I haven't touched your damned

guitar since yesterday."

"Oh, haven't you . . . I don't think . . ."

"Dirty paws yourself, then . . ." And with that I land him one good and hard. He upped and at me with clenched fist, I staggered back, right through a door that led into a passage, then measured my length, head foremost down the iron staircase. By some miracle, I escaped breaking my neck, though I had plenty of scratches as a reminder, to say nothing of a couple of black eyes.

I had had more than enough by this time. Two days later I was tossing on the high seas once more, bound for Europe. I had arrived at Buenos Aires with two thousand francs in my pocket, and was going back with thirty. Brick and I met again three months later. We made it up; but the reconciliation was only skin deep, and we parted for good three months later.

"You'll be a gone coon without me," were Brick's last words to me at parting. Well . . . when one is insulted, one can usually think of something to say . . .

24

MY WORLD PHILOSOPHY

ALL I can do to-day is to stare, and stare, and stare! It is my first visit to Holland. I have been looking at flowers, simply masses of them—and *such* flowers! I saw a garden in Hilversum full of such richness and exuberance, I could hardly tear myself away. Now I know what is wanted in my garden on the Riviera. Copper beeches! Copper beeches under an Italian sky, overlooking the Mediterranean—what a combination! I know all the famous gardens from Genoa to Hyères, and not one of them, so far as I am aware, possesses this marvellous, sombre tree. The park-keeper at Hilversum put me on to a man in Utrecht who grew trees, and from him I lately purchased a young forest of copper beeches. Also I bought tulips, ten thousand Toreador tulips, the new kind, red as a sliced-up blood orange. I shall cover that sloping ground in my garden with Toreador tulips, and the effect will be that of freshly spewed lava from a volcano.

Holland is indeed the land of water, flowers and trees. Four days ago, when I was travelling over the frontier from Bentheim, I saw the most magnificent cows in a meadow, almost as lovely as ours in the Simmental. I got out and called at the farm. The peasant was very proud of my praises and conducted me round his pasture. But it was not so simple as it sounds. For I had cut a little twig out of the hedge, and was holding it straight in front of me, and promptly felt an electric current running right through me; the soles of my feet twitched, my switch bent in a curve towards the earth, and my whole body was a prey to magnetic forces. The peasant ran and fetched a pick-axe; three times he delved, and each time water gushed out of the ground. The man went positively dippy about it.

But it is small wonder that Holland is riddled with secret springs. The strange thing is that wherever I stand I can hear them calling to me beneath my two feet. Some years ago I was the means of saving from disaster a landed proprietor in the Neuchâtel Jura, who was quite a stranger to me.

His land was simply parched for water, but we altered all that when I appeared. Last summer, when I was near Empoli, in Tuscany, I had to compel a vine-dresser, almost by force, because he was complaining to me of the dryness of his land, to dig for a spring in front of his house. When the water started to gush out of the earth, he crossed himself promptly, crooking his finger against me, with the sign that is used against the Evil Eye.

This looking for springs is the sort of thing calculated to drive a man mad. You've simply *got* to look! It's like being seized by elementals. Often, for days on end, I go ambling around my estate, holding my switch in front of me, to the despair of my family; there is an urge in me, and I simply *have* to do it. If I were to start out with my switch from Amsterdam, and make my way over the meadows, I should arrive at Haarlem like a rat-catcher, with a hundred thousand winding streams purling after me, instead of rats!

There are museums in Amsterdam with many famous pictures in them; but this doesn't mean much to me; I'm too simple for that kind of thing. I don't really see the good of painting pictures just so that they can be hung up in museums. My feelings and observation are concerned only with the artless things of life, and above all for everything that grows and has its roots within the earth. I should like to take this opportunity of painting myself in my true colours. What is Art to me, or Philosophy, either? I am no Intellectual!

All these things that get said about me are charming in their way, but they don't really wash. They are merely skilfully framed advertisements, concocted in their innocent fashion by my excellent backers. From a business point of view I can in no way complain, for an "intellectual clown" has a far greater vogue these days than does your simple-minded bucolic clown.

What is the matter with me is that I have no real—what is the comic word that the people of Berlin are so fond of using? Such a comic word that it always escapes me. For you must know, ladies and gentlemen, that I am merely *un simple Jurassien du Jura Bernois*, a simple son of the mountains, who can really only speak one language and that his mother tongue, French-Swiss—but this he can both speak and understand, and that you must place to his credit . . . Ah—now I have it . . . that comic phrase . . . *World Philosophy!* I've no World Philosophy! All the same, I know what the thing means. It means complete independence, and never being a burden on any man; that, at any rate, is what it means to me; but it's not the kind of thing I am likely to achieve by slinging long words about!

As for reading Shandy and Plutarch, I made it all up. I boasted about it, thinking it would give a nice twist to my reputation. Fancy a clown reading Plutarch! As a matter of fact, I have never heard of either Sterne's Shandy or of Plutarch. It's true I have read Corneille and Racine, and enjoyed them, too, and so far as German literature is concerned I at least know that Goethe and Schiller lived in Weimar, that Schiller wrote Tell which was afterwards set to music by Rossini, and Goethe wrote the libretto for the great Gounod's marvellous opera, *Faust and Marguerite.*

I have particularly pleasant memories of Weimar. Long before the war I was wandering through Germany with a travelling circus. One day, when we were in Zittau, our big circus tent collapsed owing to the weight of the March snow on top of it, that had fallen over-night. It was like a small earthquake; the whole place was enveloped in a swirl of dust, the shop windows cracked all around us through the shutters knocking against them, while beneath the mass of canvas struggled a confused mass of horses and their riders, for the disaster had happened during rehearsal.

The following week we were playing in Weimar. A rival of mine had surreptitiously put eggs in my square-toed shoes. When I went into the ring, half way through the bill, and began to dance, a stream of yoke of egg squelched out of every gash in my shoes. I took no notice, pretending that this "egg-dance" was merely an extra number; the audience was delighted with it. But afterwards, when I was back in my dressing-room, I had to extract my feet from a veritable omelette soufflée! And that, with your permission, is all I have to say about Weimar —*omelette soufflée!*

25

TWINS AND HUMAN TORCHES

IT makes me hot all over, only to think of U.S.A. There I saw the Yellowstone Park and the Mississippi and sailed in stormy weather on Lake Michigan, with the monstrous city of Chicago looming beneath its bank of sulphur storm-cloud. A mighty country, forsooth, but oh . . . oh . . . the drabness of the people in it and the lives they lead! New York, the Hell of Tedium!

Let me be just. My opinion might be different if I had had greater success there. I appeared in New York, Chicago and Philadelphia. But I did not make a great hit. I was too simple for the Yankees, too restrained, not enough "pep" in me. They like their turns to be allusive and full of insinuation. They like a man to be a sort of human teetotum. Above all, I was very unwell, suffering from shingles, a groggy heart and influenza. The reason for that I'll explain in a moment. I only have to land in America to attract a whole chain of calamities. Had I not already run the gauntlet in Buenos Aires? But that was a mere flea-bite to what happened in New York!

I had sailed from Liverpool, in the 22,000-ton boat *Carmenia,* and landed at Halifax. The voyage took a fortnight instead of a week. On the third day we had encountered the most appalling storm. The enormous waves seemed to reach the top even of our colossal funnels. We were driven out of our course by a thick fog. The fog-horns sounded all night long, while the wireless stations on the Canadian coast kept on sending urgent messages about the proximity of icebergs.

The more nervous passengers went to bed in their clothes, the worst pessimists of all ready with life-belts round their middles. Dinner that evening had been a most spiritless affair, and I think there was not one among us whose thoughts did not dwell on the *Titanic* disaster that had occurred some years before.

Little groups gathered where the life-boats were hung, surreptitiously calculating the amount of people each could contain, each of us trying to memorise the most advantageous

MY CHEST MUSCLES ARE SWELLING!

MY COLLAPSE—OI . . . OI . . . OI!

position to adopt. The great thing was to cotton on to those fellow-passengers whose nerves seemed best, and who could therefore be most relied on in case of danger. Myself, I had a decided predilection for a certain stalwart couple, Teddy and Daisy, brother and sister, a couple of giants known as the "fattest human beings living" who were crossing with us for a Canadian tour. Whoever froze on to Teddy and Daisy would surely never sink . . . how could they? The circumstance that these human floating docks in no way repulsed my advances, but even seemed to seek my society, was sufficient to fill my fellow passengers with envy, as well as to restore me to confidence and peace of mind.

But, towards twilight of the eighth day, the fog began to grow less thick. Visibility was better, the weather less boisterous, and all danger seemed at an end. The whole ship breathed with relief; you could positively feel how it was drawing less water, and speeding at ease once more over the watery mirror. We decided to hold a carouse, to be followed by a dance, and I was specially pressed into their service to assist.

After the evening meal, the great dining-room was converted into a concert hall, and I retired to my cabin to dress and make up.

The night was pitch dark, and the sea smooth.

I turned on the light in my cabin, removed my coat and shirt, slipped into my black tights, fitted my bald-headed wig over my hair and started to paint my face. Red mouth . . . red nose . . . and then, without one word of warning a bang went through the entire boat that brought my nose in sharp contact with my mirror All around me was a nightmare sound of clatter and clash, as though our mighty *Carmenia* was being crushed like an egg-shell. I tore open the porthole. The sea shone bright and calm under the night sky, while, in the foreground twinkled a multitude of distant lights, like a tipsily tremulous continent. There was a hissing of tremendous steam clouds. People were screeching as though their throats were being cut.

Still painted and in dishabille, I rushed into the passage-way. It was empty, of course. All the passengers were at the concert. One other door, only, was open, and in the doorway stood a lady in a pink night-dress.

"Good God, what is the matter?" she gasped, and then began to screech: "Help . . . Help" . . . at the sight of my garish, painted face. Finally she fled along the corridor as fast as her legs would take her, towards the companion, screaming the while for assistance, but at the foot of the stairs she collapsed, moaning. I hurried up to her, and saw at a glance the kind of assistance of which she was in need. I have been in my time, stable-boy, landlord, waiter, cook, washer-up, music-dealer, instrument-maker, piano-tuner, composer, fiddler, pianist, conductor, yodler, Alpine-horn blower, and clown; I have very nearly been court fool to the Sultan of Turkey; I have been instructor of foreign languages, prompter, money-taker, Holder-of-the-Book, watch-maker, gardener, fencing-master, boxer, contortionist, bull-fighter, and nursemaid. So why not midwife, for once in a way?

Anyhow, I was. With the aid of the steward, I carried the shrieking woman into the nearest cabin; the doctor was summoned, and in the midst of all the confusion attendant upon a threatened catastrophe to the ship, between us we brought into the world—that is to say the doctor did, assisted by a steward and a clown—a bouncing pair of twins. Meanwhile, the *Carmenia* had collided with the *Maryland*, but the damage incurred was only slight, and we were able to proceed cautiously on our way to Halifax, where at length we landed.

I duly fulfilled my date in that town and was then whirled off in a sleeping compartment in a train bound for New York. In the middle of the night, a fire broke out on the train. Ten killed. Four of the passengers had been telescoped amid the ruins like rats in a trap and burned to smithereens. Arrived at New York, I took a taxi. Just before reaching Madison Square, we collide with another taxi. The one I am in turns completely over, but I escape with nothing but a good fright. But the immediate result of this chain of mishaps is shingles and a heart attack, and no sooner has my time come to an end than I depart for Europe in the throes of influenza.

Quite recently, a New York manager cabled me a fabulous offer. And I, as a poor, despised European, had the hardihood to send him the following telegram by way of reply: "Am not interested in America." So you see, at long last, I have had my little revenge. Though if it interests him, I would add a rider to the following effect: if Mr. Hoover gives me personal guarantee that nothing happens to the boat I sail on, that I shall not be required to act as midwife on the journey, that my sleeping compartment on the train shall not be illuminated by the corpses of burning human beings, that the taxi that carries me through the streets of New York shall turn no single somersault, and that I shall not be laid low with either shingles, heart attack or influenza, then, good people all—why then . . . I'll come!

26

BUT I LOVE ENGLAND

AND now for England. I had had the great
clown Antonet, for a long time now, as my
partner, and together we had had triumphs
galore in France, Germany, Belgium, Hungary, Denmark and Spain. But the hardest
nut was yet to crack, in the shape of an English audience. We had heard how spoiled and
cold-blooded they all were. Colleagues had
warned us. They had told us how Londoners
sat in rows like a lot of polar bears behind a
barrier of ice. We were simply burning, now,
to tickle up these polar bears.

We had got a date at the Palace Theatre.
Antonet went on in advance to London while
I made a little trip to Paris and there bought
a car. It was the first car I had ever had, and
purchased with all cool deliberation. It cost
me far more to do it than I could really afford
—my whole capital, in fact—but I had long
made the discovery how important it was to
"bluff it" at the right moment. I have known

clowns who I may say with all conviction were every bit as good as myself—possibly better—but they just didn't know, as I did, how to hit the public eye. And that's what counts.

That it is necessary to have both talent and capacity to one's credit goes without saying. But mere capacity won't do the trick alone. It's much more important to be able to convince the world that without my talent it is incomplete. The man who is casual and easy-going and neglects these important points is simply bound to be left behind. He has no business then to grumble at the way the world has treated him. Let him rather take himself to task. I must have something within myself that compels music-hall managers to connect my name—both sides of the ocean—with the dates they simply cannot afford to lose. They must be quite convinced that without Grock every alternate year, they would be obliged to shut up shop!

Shall I tell you how it was that they paid me my first big salary—or rather how it was I forced them to pay it, and how from that moment my fame was assured? One day in Paris a manager called on me who had music-hall enterprises all over the world. I was by that time already Grock, with a popular reputation in Budapest and Madrid, as well as in Paris and Brussels, though I had not yet become the One and Only Grock . . . the World's Universal Clown.

The manager in question offered me an engagement at a rate of what he called "a nice round figure," namely five hundred francs a day. Nice round figure indeed! I should say so! I nearly died of surprise and delight. But I kept myself well in hand. I made as though I thought he had offered me eight hundred, and, cool as a cucumber I said to him, then and there, over the table: "You could have spared yourself the trouble of coming to Paris to offer me a sum of eight hundred francs a night."

Ten minutes later I had got a contract in my pocket for a thousand francs per night! Pretty good, now, wasn't it? As for my partner, I had so concentrated upon him any powers of suggestion I possessed, that he simply hadn't the nerve to correct my "mistake" due to a slight hardness of hearing!

Never show when you want anything. Let them offer you a hundred thousand without so much as moving an eyelash. Want nothing at all. There is nothing stands you in such good stead in this struggle for existence as this wanting nothing. Never for one instant let it appear that you are hard up. Being hard up is a personal offence, for the simple reason that it makes others uneasy. There is no way so sure of making others hate you as showing your poverty. I soon found that out. When I have had hunger gnawing at my stomach like a ruthless wolf, I have always pretended the whole world was at my beck and call. I have always gone about well dressed, sporting silk shirts, patent leather shoes, and fur coat, carrying an ebony walking stick with silver handle like any toff, and buying a car though it meant going without food to do it.

But we must get back to Antonet who has been waiting for me in London. The important day when I was first to appear in England drew nearer and nearer, and one morning I got into my Gregoire car to drive from Paris to London. These Londoners, I said to myself, shall see with whom they have to do, and the sort of figure I cut. All artistes were beginning to have cars then—

even the smaller fry. I had my bus safely shipped over the Channel, and once more got into it at Folkestone and proceeded to balloon off to London.

But a breakdown on the road delayed me two hours. After which I lost the way. I knew that eventually I *must* get to London: after all, the city was hardly so small that one would overlook it, but instead of entering from the South, round by the gigantic Crystal Palace, I got somehow on to a Western route by Kew Gardens. That, at any rate, is what I gathered from the unfortunate Sunday trippers whom I interrogated and to whom I could only make myself understood with the utmost difficulty. For I knew precisely one hundred and three words of English—just so many words, in fact, as the part I had learned by heart contained, and not one syllable more.

On I tooled, feeling like a needle in a bundle of hay, amid the great whirlpool of the metropolis. I had been in Berlin and I knew Paris really well; in both of these cities I could tell who I was and what I wanted; but here I felt I simply counted as nothing, and all I could do was to plunge into the hurly-burly, and make what headway I could against the current.

At one particular central spot of traffic with streets radiating out in all directions, I circled round and round in utter bewilderment till a bicyclist took pity on me and offered to guide me. He went on in front and conducted me through a medley of streets, some of them brightly lit, some almost dark, to my destination. And high time, too. There was barely an hour to run before ringing up.

This then, was the Palace Theatre, with its Renaissance frontage all picked out in dazzling lights. The Variety Artistes' names flamed out in gigantic letters. But where was *mine* flaming? *Gott strafe England!* I looked again and yet again, I peered and peered, spelling out every name in front of me, and then the crushing fact was borne in upon me that the management hadn't deemed us worthy of one single, tiny spark! I began to tremble. What had happened? Had I arrived too late? Ought I to have come the day before, and had we now been replaced in the bill? But there hung the enormous printed placard close to the entrance door, and up

I rushed to study it.

Names ... names ... a whole wilderness of names ... from large type to middling and then very small—but where was I? There were names screaming at you like a blare of trumpets, other names not quite so insistent, as it might be kettledrums, and still others more subdued like tympani. One after another I scrutinised every single letter of them, but not one sign of Grock and Antonet. Antonet and Grock, most famous clowns in all the world, what had become of you? "Piep" ... "here we are" ... "piep ... piep ... piep ..."

And so we were—the last, the very last in all the bill, as humble as you make 'em!

When I walked into our dressing-room, dear old Antonet didn't know whether to hug me or knock me down For the last twenty-four hours he had been meeting every train and enduring incredible torments, rage alternating with despair and both with resignation. Every moment he had expected our turn to be taken off. "Idiot " ... he yelled at me ... "you thundering jackass ... you double distilled ape ..."

GROCK

I let him go on, knowing it is always best to humour a man in these moods, and only lost my own temper when he began to encroach on matters personal and allude to me as "a silly Swiss cow." Now there are some things I'll not endure, and that is one of them. Like all good sons of Switzerland I am highly sensitive where any national allusions are concerned. Antonet noticed me go white with rage and stopped short in consternation. And he did well! The blaze of battle was already in my eyes, and my fingers twitched. What wouldn't I have given for a good bout of fisticuffs at that moment! But I controlled myself, for there was other work, far more important, to be done by both of us. Time was pressing and I must make up.

Our mutual interest in the show soon brought us together again. We slipped as quick as might be into our tights, slapped our wigs on to our heads, painted our mouths and noses bright red, tested our instruments, clarinet, fiddle and concertina, to see that they were all in working order, and being by this time once more the best of friends, we buried the hatchet and, standing in front of our dressing-table, gave each other one or two friendly punches in the ribs.

And now the light signal flashed through for us to go on the stage. I was as excited as anything, but so full of confidence that Antonet seemed to think it was up to him to damp my ardour by whispering:

"Don't count your chickens before they're hatched . . . London simply teems with Grocks . . ."

We stood waiting in the wings. The orchestra struck up . . . the gong clanged . . . the great moment had arrived. I started to yawn then and there so excited was I. Up went the curtain. Antonet was the first to take the stage and was received with shouts of laughter. The laughter increased tenfold when I appeared, yawning, fit to swallow a coach and horses.

"Ca y est . . . we've got 'em," whispered Antonet to me.

"I do believe we have . . ."

We could tell in a twink how the audience liked us. How different from what we had been told! In less time than it takes to tell we had established contact with them and our turn went like hot cakes; the more they clapped the funnier we were, and we were received at the end with a positive roar of applause. I chuckled to Antonet as we went off: "London's got one more Grock now, my boy!"

From that moment our names ceased to hide their diminished heads on the bill. Our contract was promptly increased by six weeks. We actually appeared at the Palace for ten weeks on end. After which we contracted with the other big music halls, the Alhambra and the Empire, though the most important of them all, the Coliseum, that dream and Mecca of all variety artistes, still seemed able to do without us.

One evening I stood by the Nelson column in Trafalgar Square, looking enviously up at the name of the great Fregoli blazing over the roof of the Coliseum, in gigantic letters. What if it were Grock, thought I, instead of Fregoli? One day, of course, it would be. And so it was, for three years later, almost to a day, my name was shining in the identical place where Fregoli's had shone. I could see it like a beacon from ever such a long way off. For five consecutive Christmases the Coliseum gave Londoners a Christmas present of Grock. The Spirit of Christmas hovered over the building, picked out in large lights, and this Spirit of Christmas would flutter down to earth bearing Grock upon its back.

My great London success was an open sesame to me for all the provincial music-halls. The two of us went on tour to Glasgow, Manchester, Liverpool, Leeds, Sheffield and Birmingham to the tune of sixty pounds a week. When I returned to these towns a couple of years later I was received with a frenzy of acclamations. But, alas, it was not with Antonet. By that time I had another partner.

I was having consistently bad luck with my partners, whom I kept having to change. One of them religiously drank himself stiff before every show; another, who was an excellent fiddler, was such a victim to stage fright you never knew when he was going to be sick. I have had the most appalling narrow escapes with him on one stage after another, always having to watch him, poor fellow, and facilitate his exit at the necessary moment, if required. I remember one evening at the Alhambra in Glasgow, in particular, when I literally had to cuff him off the boards to avert the threatened catastrophe. The audience roared with laughter, little knowing.

The next partner I worked with was an Italian. He too was a good fiddler, but surly, and clumsy as an elephant. I used to be dreadfully put off by his buccaneer moustache.

"Cut it off," I exhorted him one day.

"I don't choose to."

Later on I repeated the request. But the rascal's only reply was to shake his fist in my face. I shut up and said nothing. But one evening in Manchester, just before the show, when my elephant was occupied with both hands, making up, I slipped my right arm, quick as lightning, round his head, while with my left . . . snip . . . snap . . . I cut one side of his moustache off . . .

It proved a positive inspiration. Like the more famous Samson, my giant suddenly lost all his strength and roughness. He became gentle and docile, himself picking up the scissors with a smile, and shearing off the other half to match. But, bereft of his virile adornment, from this moment he suffered both from stage fright and sluggish memory, and I had to get rid of him. But the legal claim he tried to bring against me for compensation for damages was dismissed.

27

TOMATOES IN PETERSBURG

THE London Coliseum is for music-hall artistes what the stage of the Milan Opera House is for an opera singer. A variety artiste is made for life once he appears on the boards of the Coliseum.

The Scala and also the Winter Garden at Berlin are magnificent places on a huge scale. But the actual stage-room at the Coliseum is equal to the whole of the Scala. Four turns, all prepared, are always ready and waiting on the huge revolving stage. So huge is it, I have actually seen a horse race take place on it.

The first time I appeared there was in very distinguished company. No less than nine international celebrities shared the bill with me. The management had placed me at the top, making my turn come first. On the Continent, this first turn is always regarded as something of a stop-gap, and for this reason I wasn't best pleased, though I ought to have known that in England the first item on the programme is practically as good as any other. I remembered too, how in professional circles the Coliseum is known as the "Comedians' Graveyard." A clown has jolly well got to have something in him before he can fill this enormous space with his own exploits and personality.

But all went far beyond my expectations. The applause was so hearty, and lasted such a long time, that the second turn had to come on late. The newspapers were in a positive ecstasy. One notice in particular from *The Times* made my heart go pit-a-pat. I felt prouder than Punch or any peacock, and was full of the feeling: "I have gone to the head of the whole of London . . . all London is thinking of me and nothing but me . . . they whisper about me in corners . . . they dig one another in the ribs, and whisper the great question: HAVE YOU SEEN HIM? And who is HIM? Why—Grock, of course!

I once played at the Coliseum for twenty-five weeks on end—six months, in fact. Let me spread myself a little on my English reminiscences! Let me indulge in a little retrospective boasting about the popularity I enjoyed and still enjoy in England! It is some years now since I made my last appearance there. But here before me is a child's letter from Manchester. Evidently there is something in the English papers about my playing at Amsterdam. Could I not possibly put in a hurried trip across the Channel? I am deeply touched. Who'd have thought of there being a kiddies' paper published in English, still printing snippy bits about Grock, how he is, and what he is doing!

I am more than a little crazed on everything English. I like the breed of men they are, their manner of upbringing, their eternal haphazardness, their tolerance, their healthy dislike of being made fools. I can't do anything but praise them. By now I have had the opportunity of cogitating on the peoples of many lands. And this is the conclusion I have come to—that we could all do very much worse than mould ourselves according to English principles! I know what I am talking about. I was in Russia, for instance, shortly before the war broke out. Not since, though.

The thought of an engagement to play in Soviet Russia tempts me not at all. Far from it. Some foreign colleagues of mine were recently doing so, and what do you suppose happened to them? They were arrested, every one of them, for sending complimentary seats to some Russian friends of theirs, when playing in a circus in a Southern Russian town. The recipients of the seats were arrested, too, and all concerned subjected to a most painful examination. It is strictly against the law to send free seats—smacks too much of individualism, is altogether anti-social, and inimical to that sacrosanct monster the *State!* Russian circuses are a State enterprise, and the Russian clowns and trick-riders and acrobats and fire-eaters, State servants, every one of 'em! You can't turn a somersault without its being a State gesture! As for your comic artiste he is liable to get himself clapped into prison almost before opening that big red mouth of his, on suspicion of trying to make the State ridiculous, and if he repeats the offence as likely as not it will end in his death.

Anybody seeing Moscow and Petersburg before the outbreak of war, could feel that something terrible was brewing. I arrived at Moscow on the 15th May, 1914. I had just been fulfilling a date in Vienna at the Apollo. I only knew enough Russian to serve the requirements of my programme, a Russian having translated my part for me during the railway journey. I found the horses simply wonderful, but everything else around me seemed rotten, absolutely rotten and reeking as a dung-hill. In the midst of the present, like an invisible presence, was the future infecting the whole atmosphere.

Let me tell you first about Petersburg. Never before had I seen such a beautiful, magnificent city. Whole streets full of palaces. Could one but peep through their windows! I got the briefest of glances through a chink in the curtains, and that was quite enough for me! I was playing in one of the smartest music-halls in the town, the Villa Rode. It *was* smart, too, and no mistake—the audience consisted exclusively of members of the aristocracy, military officers of highest rank, and dignitaries of the Civil Service.

One evening in particular do I remember, and with good reason, for it was the 23rd of June, the day after the murder at Serajevo. Some General or other was celebrating his

Jubilee. The theatre bristled with decorated officers and half-naked women. There must have been a pretty conglomeration of human flesh assembled there together, reduced to weights and measures! And this mass of human flesh was screaming and roaring and singing all together with unabated energy for hours on end. The great thing was to shy champagne bottles at the tall pier glasses that lined the walls all round. The glasses would be shattered to smithereens with much noise, after which the buffet would be besieged. Pies and poultry would be sent flying across space, and jammy tarts stuck to the surface of the mirrors. While I, meanwhile, stood before the footlights, trying to perform!

My performance soon resolved itself into nothing but skilfully dodging the tarts and pies that were being hurled at me. Suddenly something squidgy sloshed me in the face. I had noticed the eminent officer with the fat red face and little grey turn-up moustaches, going over to the buffet and collecting a plateful of tomatoes. We were the objective of those same tomatoes, but to begin with they missed me, every one, falling to the right and left of my face, till one of them hit me plump on my forehead. Tears of caviare coursed down my cheeks, and my nose dripped mayonnaise salad. My success was colossal. One of the waiters told me the General's name. It was General N——, whom later on the Bolsheviks were said to have shot.

The declaration of war found me in Riga, playing at the Casino. I caught a boat to Copenhagen, in which city I sat tight for a whole fortnight, and by the middle of August was in Berlin. The Germans were marching on Paris! A week later I reported at Bienne and offered myself for the Swiss Frontier Service.

28

MY COLLEAGUE ANTONET

VIENNA. Let me first tot up the number of words. Surely I'm nearly through? Here we go—fifty-six thousand four hundred and twenty-seven! That leaves another thirteen thousand six hundred and ninety-three! How shall I fill in? Reminiscences . . . passages of conversation . . . and tarradiddles! If it's all the same to my readers, I'll betake me to Spain, now. But first of all I must tell you about Antonet, my old partner and friend who went there with me, and helped to undermine the land of Spain with me. It's half-past seven now. Antonet will be sitting in his dressing-room at the Cirque de Paris, making up for the evening show. If his ears aren't burning, they ought to be!

The public has a rooted idea that all you have to do in order to become a clown is to practise a whole week long every morning in front of the glass, rolling your eyes and putting out your tongue as far as it will go. A

tongue and a looking glass are certainly part
of a clown's outfit, and by no means to be
despised, either of them, but a long tongue
and a big mouth no more go to complete a
clown than a paint brush does an artist or
horn-rimmed spectacles a poet. No clown can
be a real clown without the help of tradition
and method, and an exhaustive technical
training for his profession.

Your clown, just as much as any other
artist, is the product of tradition. Just as a
painter knows how to use the experience of
countless forerunners, just as an author who
is an author largely owes his existence to the
pioneer work of those who have gone before
and influenced him, so every clown that is
worth his salt is but carrying on the torch
handed to him by all the eminent clowns who
preceded him or who work with him still.
Your painter will swear by Raphael, or
Calame, or Stuck as the case may be, your
author by Paul de Kock, Goethe, or Edgar
Wallace, while your clown will acknowledge
his debt to Bébé and Serillo, or Pippo and
Toniloff, or Toto, or Willi and Adolf Ols-
chonski, or La Water Lee, or Gobert Belling,
or Les Briators, or Rico and Alex, or Seiffer,

or Carlo and Mariano, or Little Walter, or Averino Antonio, or the three Fratellini, or Antonet.

Umberto Guilleaume, who goes by the name of Antonet, a leading clown of the Cirque de Paris, was my teacher. He comes of a famous Italian clown family. I was the bud, so to say, that burst into bloom beneath the rays of Antonet's sun. The day I got to know him in Buenos Aires was the most important day of my life, professionally speaking. I had just fought myself to a frazzle with Brick, and Antonet was as ill-suited with his partner as I was with mine. We were both engaged by the same circus and saw one another for the first time at a rehearsal in the briefest fashion. But after it was over we got together, and simultaneously spoke out what was in our minds:

"We must join forces. I'm on contract for the time being, but directly I'm free I'll work with you!"

For a whole year we lost sight of one another, but each was thinking of the other and quite convinced that this association was inevitable and would surely come to pass. One day I was in Madrid. I had just had a blazing row with Brick who had been appearing with me at the Pelotario, with Raquel Meller in the same bill. I walked along the Puerta del Sol where the crowds are thickest, wondering what on earth to do, and thinking hard of Antonet. If only I knew where he had got to! Should I just go off to Paris and look for him there? Suddenly a hand was laid on my shoulder. Who was it, do you suppose? Antonet!

"I've been looking for you!"

"And I—for you!"

He had arrived that very day to fulfil an engagement at the Circo Parish, with his same old partner. But their contract was now just ending, and they were playing together for the last time.

"I am living in Marseilles," he told me. "I've a studio in my house. Come along and work with me there."

We worked for three solid months together in Marseilles, putting in fifteen hours per day and frequently working through the night as well. Antonet put me thoroughly through my paces in music, miming and acrobatics, and was inexhaustible with his excellent advice and ideas. He literally polished me up to the

nines. We tackled one instrument after another, till our arms almost dropped from our
bodies through sheer tiredness; we practised
the fiddle, the clarinet, the piano, the drum,
the hurdy-gurdy and the concertina. Though
I says it as shouldn't, I am one of the best
concertina performers going to-day. Nothing
could have been stricter, if we had been pre-
paring for a Government exam. After that
we drew up our programme and tried various
circus entrances together. There was the
famous Serenade to Marietta, since become
a circus classic, and alluded to in my first
chapter, " A Royal Confinement." There
was Kubelik and Rubinstein. There was
the entrance with the twenty instruments.
Our turns were really more than circus
turns, being sketches, or small pieces suit-
able for the theatre—a fact that an English
court of law later confirmed on my behalf,
when I was forced to sue a fellow for plagi-
arism who, if left to his own sweet will,
would doubtless be masquerading under my
feathers to this day on the variety stage.

I think Antonet and myself can justly
pride ourselves on having raised the clown's
profession to a higher level and made it more

respected. We opened up new paths, and showed that the clown can be a great deal more than just Silly Hans, running after the Ring Master in the intervals, bumping his nose into the lights. A good clown, these days, can occupy every bit as high a position as a good actor. He is practising an art.

We now signed a contract with the Circo Allegria in Barcelona at 1,800 pesetas per month for the two of us. The unqualified success of our dress rehearsal at the Cirque Cayol in Marseilles put considerable heart into us, though it did not make us over-confident, for we knew we were about to be subjected to a considerable test. For Spain is the Land of Clowns, just as Italy is the Land of Tenors. The judgment of a Spanish audience on circus matters is highly critical and expert, and of international importance for professional purposes. If a clown can please the Spaniards then he can please anybody. Their critics will only praise circus performances that are really first-rate. World competition is merciless. At our first appearance at the Circo Allegria we had four other pairs of clowns up against us. These rascals had clubbed together against us, all eight of them, and thought of a most scoundrelly way to try and do us down. I had a sort of premonition, and went on in advance to Barcelona in order to see the kind of programme that they were getting ready to put in the ring against us. The rogues had quite obviously been employing a spy in Marseilles, who had already pinched on their behalf several of our best ideas for them to mix with their turn. We had to let it go through for the first performance, but after that we completely diddled them by setting them on a false track. We rehearsed all that morning in the ring, laboriously going through a number for all to see —but we did not include it in the evening's programme. We had meanwhile prepared a far better turn that we had worked on in private behind closed doors in a room we had hired for the purpose. No amount of hissing and whistling on the part of our rivals could prevent Antonet and Grock from becoming the topic of the hour by the end of a week. The whole town was agog to see us.

29

THE ORDEAL OF DRINK

THE inhabitants of Barcelona were positively ravished by my "porker's phiz." A porker's phiz à la Grock became all the rage: several of my colleagues have adopted it to this day.

These Spanish rivals of ours forced Antonet and myself to invent some novelty at every show. Nothing was ever more sudden than this particular inspiration of mine. One evening, sitting at my dressing-table, fitting my bald wig tight over my own hair, I thought to myself: "NO. This artificial baldness is unworthy of you!" On which I deliberately sacrificed my own romantic locks, shearing them off inexorably with the cutters: after that I ran over my head with a sharp razor blade till not a semblance of a hair was left on my bald pate that looked for all the world like the pigs' heads butchers adorn their windows with, with a lemon stuffed into the mouth. My readers really should have seen

me then, complete with vermilion nose and mouth! With my little grey hat balanced on top of my head I wambled into the ring, with an embarrassed smile on my face!

Our season at Barcelona extended to six months. Our reputation spread far and wide, and a whole heap of towns were after us.

First of all we went on to Saragossa with the Allegria Troupe. The fame that had preceded us brought an audience of twenty thousand to our opening performance. Antonet and I were in the middle of the bill that began with Pippo and Andreff, another pair of clowns. I was looking on, concealed, when they made their entrance—and a good thing, too, for Andreff had stolen my porker's phiz idea, every inch of it. The audience simply roared when he entered the ring, playing off *my* notion on them! I was within an ace of leaping into the ring myself, for sheer rage, but Antonet restrained me, and after a moment's consideration I hurried back to my dressing-room. When the music for our turn began, I made my appearance covered all over with tiny, painted hairs of a foxy red, that I had painted on to my bald pate right down to the back of my neck, one by one. *Success?* Aha—it needs a stronger word than that to describe it!

We were in need of whole baskets in which to collect the cigars and "puros" that were flung at us from every side. On one particular giant cigar we flung ourselves like a couple of vultures.

"L'ho visto el primo!" I called out to Antonet, and the audience held its sides with laughter, looking up at the big box occupied by the gentleman who had flung the cigar at me and who seemed to be laughing most of all. I wanted to say that I had been the first to see it, which apparently should have been: "L'ho visto el primero!" "L'ho visto el primo" being interpreted meant: "I've seen the silly ass!" And the silly ass and donor of the giant cigar was no less a person than the Alcalde, the Mayor of Saragossa!

We simply hadn't got enough arms to collect all the " botas" or leathern skins filled with wine that the delighted spectators proceeded to hurl at us from their seats. We found that it was up to us to break off and toss off the wine then and there in great gulps, head well thrown back, and then to toss the skins back again to where they came from. Had we failed to drink one single drop we should have been shamed for ever, but we showed them that we were stout fellows, equal to the occasion, and would often undergo this ordeal as much as twelve times in one evening, with such success that our audience were even more elated with us after we had drunk than before.

In short we were friends with our audience. Times out of number they carried us off to hunt rabbits with them or go off on a binge and, as often as not, when we would try and settle up accounts at whatever public house or café we had been to, the waiter or proprietor would make a deprecatory gesture: "No, indeed, gentlemen . . . no . . . no . . . indeed—it's all been paid for!"

So much for life in Saragossa!

But how poor and inadequate language seems for trying to convey all this effervescence and generosity, and how flat it all sounds, set down on paper!

The day came when we packed up, lock, stock and barrel, tents, scenery, costumes, drums, trumpets, fiddles, monkeys, bears, sea-lions, and one monstrous elephant that weighed as much as all the rest of us put to-

gether, and took boat for Valencia. And
what a boat—an antiquated old steamer in
which we set off for the Balearic Islands like
the Ark of Noah, rocking on the waves. It
all sounds very pleasant and amusing, no
doubt, but if I could but give you any idea of
what it was *really* like . . . Words fail me,
again.

It was the middle of January, and the
weather as warm and mild as it is with us in
the North at the beginning of September.
The journey very nearly started with a catastrophe, for no sooner had the elephant
clumped on board than he was in danger of
capsizing the boat through his extreme
avoirdupois. He had taken up a position too
near the end of the ship, and our people only
averted disaster by rushing to the other end
with the utmost presence of mind, thereby
establishing equilibrium. We weighed anchor
and the elephant was duly installed and
tethered along by the captain's bridge. With
such a considerable ballast as that in the
centre of things we thought we could surely
defy wind and weather; but there wasn't
any to defy, for the sea kept still as a duck-
pond, and looked to be made of air, rather

than water, an air of blue and peace both above us and below us, as we serenely made our course to the Balearic Isles. True, a sudden panic seized us before we had got very far, owing to an unexpected jerk of the ship. A collision? Oh, no. Only that our elephant had got tired of standing and lain down.

For two weeks on end we played in Palma de Mallorca, and in our off-time we would lie basking beneath the palm trees, bathing and fishing, and taking the fish we had caught in with us to the eating houses we frequented, where we would have them fried and served up with good, heady wine, shared amid friends. For of friends there was no lack. Nothing would have pleased the Alcalde of Palma better than concluding a contract with us for the rest of our natural lives, but Continental engagements would not be denied, and the troupe must needs depart. Our old sea-tub turned up again from Valencia, according to programme. The tents were struck and men and beasts embarked. Amid much singing and waving of handkerchiefs the boat with its gaily-coloured cargo stood out again to sea.

But Antonet and I had severed our connection with this circus. The very next day we started off in a sailing boat for Minorca for a whole month's holiday. Oh, when did ever clown have such a good time as we did then?

Four weeks of springtide holiday in Minorca . . . four glorious weeks of bathing and lazing, eating good fish and drinking good wine and wandering up hill and down dale! And working, into the bargain. We made an intensive study of the "zarzuella," and got many a musical notion for new turns from the lovely, old Spanish melodies. We would practise our turns every day in secluded spots on the lonely sea-shore. Antonet would go in front with his guitar and I would follow him, singing and dancing, while the little fishes would pop their heads out of the water and make goo-goo eyes at us.

30

ON THE HORNS OF A DILEMMA

Our "Sarsuella" was an unprecedented success in the Circo Parish at Madrid. So rich a harvest had we brought back from our holiday in Minorca that we were able to change our programme every evening. Our stock of properties and costumes was increasing rapidly now. Already we could fill thirty-four baskets.

The fame of our Spanish triumphs had spread far beyond the Pyrenees, and managers and agents were making us alluring offers for Paris, Brussels and Berlin. But to each and all of them we said "no." We simply couldn't tear ourselves away from this lovely, care-free country of Spain. There was something so *unanimous* about it and its people, something so free of all pretence. They would never applaud us in the ring, only to disparage us outside. As I have already mentioned, we would have an audience of twenty thousand gathered together

to see us with their shouts of Olee . . .
Olee . . .! That meant that next day we had
twenty thousand friends more to our credit.
Wherever we went, friendly hands were
stretched out to greet us and draw up chairs
for us to sit on. Nothing would do but that
we must eat with our friends . . . drink with
them . . . and generally jollify with them . . .

This attitude of unbuttoned cordiality
suited me to a T, for I am not at all the kind
of man who wants to make merry only in the
circus, and for the rest of his time goes about
like any ordinary citizen, stolid and self-
contained. My attitude has always been that
if I am a clown in the ring I can and should
be a clown out of the ring. Either you should
be a thing or *not* be it. That always has been,
and still is, one of my most rooted convic-
tions, and I lived up to it in Spain, to the perpetual delight of all concerned.

What we wanted more than anything else
was to have our own circus and do our own
turns in it.

"I have what we are looking for." Antonet
one day announced, beaming. A cousin of
his, the manager of a travelling circus, had
apparently read about us in the Spanish

papers. We didn't wait for a second invitation but set off there and then to see him. His name was Volsi and he was only a day's journey away.

We met him, together with his circus, at Villafranca de los Baros. Volsi had spared no pains to broadcast our fame—so much so that the local inhabitants simply didn't believe him. The greatest clowns in all the world to be appearing in Villafranca de los Baros! Surely there was a catch somewhere. The result was that on the opening night the tent, which should have held a thousand people, was only half full. However, we did not let this daunt our spirits, but gave the audience of our very best, and by the end of the show they were simply eating out of our hands.

A host of new friends escorted us to where we were putting up. We awoke next morning, early, to the sound of fresh applause. I am inclined to think, even, that it was *not* fresh applause, but that they had stood beneath our window all night, with hoarse cries of *Olee* . . . *Olee* . . . while we had been wrapped in slumber. Up we got and advanced to the window in our night-shirts. Tumultuous applause and enthusiasm. They proceeded to throw things at us—flowers, a good garlic sausage, cigarettes and a newspaper. It was the local journal with an extra supplement printed in the middle containing an exhaustive account of our exploits!

On we went, from one small town to another. I can only say these good, simple folk took us two arch simpletons to their hearts. At length we reached Almendralejo in Estremadura.

Almendralejo! For me there is no more magical word. Gentle reader, conjure up all the best words you have ever heard, into your mind: warm-heartedness, cheerfulness, mirth, exuberance, sympathy, and you have them all in Almendralejo! Quite recently, a countryman of mine just back from a Spanish tour, told me they still remembered us in Almendralejo. Grandmama and Grandpapa were still telling the young fry about the two clowns, Grock and Antonet, who turned the whole town topsy-turvy for the space of two days, and completely captured all hearts.

When we first arrived there, everything happened much in the ordinary way. After we had given our show in the Bull Ring there would be a procession through the town amid the plaudits of the crowd, and then we would be received in the shady precincts of some stately noble's house; next day we would be invited to a hunting party, that would probably include various other secret adventures of a more sentimental nature—and all of this in a positively tropical climate, with the thermometer standing at 130 degrees, on one occasion!

But an incident occurred that stirred up general sympathy in our favour. We had engaged the town band of Almendralejo to play for us every evening for 35 pesetas a night. One day the conductor announced they would be unable to play for us next night, owing to another engagement, unless we paid double salaries. In fact, unfair extortion. How on earth could we replace them in the time? I had a sudden inspiration. I got hold of a pal and bade him ride hell for leather to Villafranca de los Baros, and bring back from there the town band that had played for us during our visit. I felt sure they'd come.

All our friends were with us to a man, and regarded the behaviour of their local musicians as a disgrace to the town. The sun was setting when our recruits from Villafranca arrived in a carriage and four, smothered in dust, and were acclaimed on the spot as heroes. Their arrival was heralded by trumpet and drum. All our Almendralejo partisans headed the procession; then came the musicians in their carriage, in which rode both Antonet and myself, with colossal sombrero hats upon our heads, flinging copper coins amid the multitude as we passed on our triumphal way. Deliberately we paraded through the great Square where the local band was already at work. And now the welkin rang with the fanfare of trumpets; their sharp tones stabbed like knives through the air, till the clouds of the evening sky were torn to shreds, and at length the extortioners were obliged to knuckle under with all due humiliation to their merciless rivals from Villafranca, secure in the possession, not only of right on their side, but of the general sympathy of the crowd.

Our recruits proved themselves the ideal circus band. We pressed them to stay on another day and yet another, and then a third and then a fourth—and by the time the fifth day came round we positively could not do without them. For we had thought of something tremendously novel in the way of a turn: something, surely, never yet attempted by any clown on earth. A bull-fight! I had always gone to see bull-fights whenever I could, in Barcelona, Madrid, Saragossa, Granada and Seville, and the wild, wonderful, dangerous sport had almost intoxicated me. Ever since I had wanted to have a shot at it myself, to do some bull-fighting on my own, a mock fight, be it understood, conducted as a clown would. The project began to shape when one night after the show a breeder of bulls called on us with the announcement that he had a young bull to dispose of at a very special price, 65 pesetas. Antonet already knew something about the sport: he had appeared as a toreador more than once, and distinguished himself by his fine appearance and swift decision.

But Volsi, our manager, would have nothing to do with the notion. He said the toreadors of Estremadura would never tolerate rivalry of that sort, especially with clowns to supplant them. It would be poking fun at the national sport of Spain and

Photo. Stone, Berlin

THIS IS MY DEAR WIFE

I DON'T LIKE WRITING IN THE HEAT

making it ridiculous. He prophesied a
scandal of infinite magnitude. Very well.
We decided to take on the project at our own
risk and expense, once having secured the
willing assistance of our colleagues in the
ring.

We had a bill printed in Saragossa, about
as large as half a Swiss Canton. We then
put on our clowns' kit, loaded the huge bills
on to a hand-cart, and plastered them all,
with gigantic, dripping brushes, on every
available coign of vantage in the town. We
announced a sports programme: a four hundred metre race for amateurs; a donkey
race; a sack race for children from four to
eight, a raffle with a fat pig as prize, and
finally a fight between ourselves and a couple
of bulls, one of which would be killed. The
black pig had been given to us by an admirer,
one of the bulls was merely hired for a sham
fight, while the other, destined for death, we
had purchased ourselves, as I have already
related.

This great event was fixed for a Sunday,
but by the previous Friday Almendralejo
was seized with a fever of expectation, nobody could do any more work, the children

were given a holiday from school, and from
morning to night the streets were filled with
expectant idlers, crowding into the principal
Square where the music was playing. Whenever we appeared in our clown's oufit—and
we kept it on now the entire day—we were
met with the most tremendous enthusiasm.
As for the old house in which we were stay-
ing, it was as though transformed into the
headquarters of some impending battle.
Friends and supporters both from country
and town would call on us as though ex-
pressly to receive our last instructions and
commands, while among them came and
went deputies from the local clubs and
neighbouring villages: the native "toreros"
protested their loyalty towards us, while we
clowns throughout it all sat on our trunks
and received all this homage with a roguish
sort of *"grandezza."* Our faithful adherents,
waiting in the Square below, could hear the
volleys of laughter that came from the room
we sat in. Even the Alcalde waited upon us,
much as the commander of an occupied for-
tress waits upon those who have stormed it.
And why not? We really had taken this
town by storm, and called upon it to sur-

render unconditionally to our merry mood
and joyous command.

Arrived Sunday, a scorching hot day beneath a broiling sky. The whole town was
up and doing from earliest morning, and the
amphitheatre was besieged with spectators
long before the show was timed to begin. A
cloud of dust could be seen forming in the
distance, concealing the hundreds of peasants trailing in on foot or else in their little
carts. At length an audience assembled of
twenty-five thousand. The authorities, together with the Alcalde, sat in the places of
honour, with the Justice of the Peace at their
head.

The show began at two in the afternoon.
We opened with a procession round the ring,
Antonet riding a donkey and myself perched
on the prize pig that was wreathed in gar-
lands for the occasion, our cavalcade of
assistants galloping after us on Anda-
lusian stallions made of pasteboard. Our
audience rose to a man and shouted with
glee, while we suffered our first bombard-
ment of hats, cigarettes and copper coins.
We proceeded according to programme. The
racers contested for their prize; the donkey

bucked and jibbed and duly discarded its riders, while young and old enjoyed the delights of a sack race. Everything went merrily enough, though the spectators were all of them still in a state of suspense, waiting impatiently till it was time for the bullfight. In fact, such was their condition of expectation that the winner of the pig actually forgot to claim his prize! The animal was dispatched several days afterwards in the midst of the ring, cooked then and there on the spot and eaten by all and sundry down to the very tip of its tail with infinite satisfaction.

And now a blare of trumpets announced the great stunt. The picadors, with their enormous caricatures of pikes, waltzed in on their pasteboard steeds, followed by the toreadors, the matador and his deputy the *Sobre Saliente*. Antonet and I were the matador and the Sobre Saliente.

Antonet was fantastically rigged out as a combination of Bajazzo and toreador, and I sported my big floppy-toed shoes that I always wore, my white shirt-front, and black chimney-pot hat. I pretended to be dreadfully nervous of the crowd, and still more terrified of the wild beasts about to be let loose on us, clinging like a leech to Antonet's coat tails, in desperation.

The sign was now given by the Alcalde flinging the keys of the bull's cage, or *torillo*, into the ring. The keeper undid the door and out stepped a bull, magnificent to look at but wholly devoid of temperament; a most sheepish sort of animal that took a couple of hesitating steps forward and then stood stock still. My simulated fright really *was* alarm, for to have a great beast like that with its pair of colossal horns only three paces from your own body really is an uncomfortable sensation. I thought of all the blood I had seen shed on previous occasions; already I could feel those relentless horns probing into my very vitals, as I concealed myself discreetly, top-hat and all, behind Antonet. But the bull regarded us, mooneyed as any calf, and never budged an inch. The picadors, having changed their pasteboard horses for real ones, rode up and prodded it; Antonet flapped his red cloth, the *muleta* rapped it on the nose, and the bull stood there, licking its lips.

"Eh, la vacca!" the gallery shouted down,

bitterly disappointed.

"Go on, Adrien," whispered Antonet to me.

"Good God—what d'you want me to do?"

"Seize hold of it of course, you idiot . . ."

The audience was beginning to whistle in derision. I breathed a cursory prayer, and with all the courage of despair grabbed the bull by its tail and pulled it backwards. That did the trick. The bull made a sudden bound forward and began to run; it ran more than I'd bargained for; and not having let go of the tail quick enough I was dragged half round the ring after it, willy nilly. Off flew my stove-pipe hat from my head. I stumbled along as best I could, and, letting go suddenly, turned a somersault and landed flat on my back, to the delectation of all spectators. They yelled with delight. Antonet, meanwhile, with much dexterity, had stuck a couple of "banderillos" in the beast's neck and the encounter was over.

The bull was trundled back to the *torillo* and was succeeded by the other one with which we really meant business. This was a wicked-looking thick-set sort of brute, that had been kept in the dark two days on end, this being a method of making bulls fiercer and harder to tackle. It stood still, first, being blinded by the bright light. That's when you do the Don Tancredo stunt. Do you know what that means, gentle reader? It means standing straight in front of the bull, and never flickering with an eyelash when it prepares to rush at you.

Your motionless attitude makes an impression on it—or should do. At the last moment it will stop short and swerve aside. But woe unto you if you can't keep yourself still, or try to run away. Once that happens you're done.

The air was throbbing with heat. The amphitheatre was like nothing so much as a gigantic dovecot full of the fluttering of doves' wings, the wings being the fans with which the women tried to cool themselves. My black garments were sticking to me like a bathing suit, so hot and perspiring was I. My white shirt-front seemed stuck on me like a baby's bib, and my make-up ran in sanguinary smears all the length of my face. But I stood there, inwardly praying, and doing the Don Tancredo business, once . . . twice . . . three times. Each time the bull ran at me full tilt with lowered head and then stopped short at the critical moment.

I now began to be foolhardy, and with a bound seized the brute by the tail, hauling myself up on to his back and landing with a double somersault in the ring again on my own back. Up I got, again confronting my quarry, with a low bow hanging my top-hat on one of its horns. The bull butted at me but missed and ran against the *muleta,* held out to him by Antonet. But gradually the brute refused to be enticed by Antonet or his *muleta;* it was foaming now with rage, stamping and snorting in my wake; I could feel its hot breath on the seat of my trousers.

The *estrade* . . . The *estrade* . . . Multitudes of helping hands were stretched out for me to grasp . . . not a fan flickered now . . . the arena was so still you could have heard a pin drop . . . But before the bull had managed to impale me from behind I had swung myself over the *estrade* and was making a long nose at it. The seat of my trousers had suffered considerably, none the less; those devilish horns had torn a mighty rent across them, and torn more than that, too. I could feel the blood beginning to ooze

through the wound. But once again I leapt into the arena, dancing around like a cat on hot bricks, both hands on my injured part, and the audience simply adored me for it.

Meanwhile the bull was exhausted and done for, and the fight came to its appointed end in the approved fashion. Antonet strode up to the Box of Honour and called out for all to hear: "Señor Alcalde, I crave your permission to dispatch the bull. If I don't do the business properly, then the *coletta* shall be shorn from my head!" (The *coletta* is the symbolical pigtail worn by all toreadors.)

My colleague now proceeded with the most expert skill to lure the bull by means of the *muleta* into the desired position; there stood the trembling victim before him, the two front hooves close together, and head lowered for a last despairing onslaught. In a trice the *spada* had been driven between the shoulder-blades up to the hilt. Antonet plucked the dagger out of the wound, and the black blood came dripping after it. The bull sank on to its knees, and an assistant gave it its final death-blow behind the ear.

GROCK

And now the audience once for all let themselves go in wildest enthusiasm. The space betwixt the amphitheatre and the ring was fairly filled with flying objects; wineskins positively rained down upon us; we picked them up, and after drinking their contents tossed them back again to the throwers; hats were hurled at us, one after another; and I ran and collected them as they fell, putting them all on my head before flinging them back again. It rained showers of cigarettes, and we were bombarded on all sides with copper coins and pesetas. The amount of gold coins we picked off the floor was enough to fill three huge baskets.

A triumphal procession was already beginning to form in the arena. Six stout men carried the baskets in front under police protection; then came Antonet and myself, carried on our admirers' shoulders. The applause was enough to bring the very houses tumbling about our ears, and the populace shouted itself hoarse beneath our windows for a sight of us. Over and over again they called for us. But we were busy, with the help of seven assistants, counting the great heap of coins and doing it up into bundles. This pleasant task took us the whole night and lasted till seven o'clock next morning. Our audience had flung into the arena no less a sum than eight thousand, seven hundred pesetas.

31

A MINIATURE END OF THE WORLD

MUNSTER in Westphalia! Viva San Luigi di Gonzaga, my great emprise is almost ended! Sixty-nine thousand, one hundred and twenty-seven words! Another eight hundred and seventy-three and it is finished according to contract! And what's more, it *shall* be according to contract, and not one syllable more, even if I have to break off in the middle of a line! I'm a hard nut in business, as I've told you before, and always ready to shake my fist in my partner's face, but nobody can say I am not pernickety and correct—correct to a T.

Münster is curiously sinister and beautiful. A native of the city, of a Sadist turn of mind, took much relish in telling me how, four hundred years ago, the dead bodies of the Anabaptists were hung in three cages on the top of the Lamberti Tower, the flesh being torn from the bones by swarms of predatory birds till nothing was left but the skeletons.

I was making an excellent meal, while he told me the story, in a certain café that had once been an old nobleman's dwelling, where another incredible personage, that crazy fellow Bomberg, had lived his life, so full of splendour and activity. There's a man I'd like to have known.

I have been feeling almost Bombergian myself during the time of my engagement here at the Schützenhof. Behold me sitting beneath the magnificent chestnut trees, drinking my beer, with my wife at my side working at her embroidery. I thought there could be no such beautiful chestnut trees anywhere as ours at Bienne.

What is this noise of shooting going on behind me? Bang . . . bang . . . bang . . . one after another, just like a real Swiss shooting contest! I cannot resist the dear, familiar sounds, and opening a private door I enter the courtyard. One side of it is taken up by the shooting stand, in front of which at a distance of two hundred metres six targets are placed. The opposite side of the courtyard is occupied by a little Biedermeier house. On the verandah belonging to this little house is a big table on which is placed a bowl of punch as large as the scalloped basin of any Roman fountain, around which are seated the competitors, half a dozen old gentlemen, drinking and smoking, and all of them replete with comfort and good cheer. They empty their glasses to the last drop, knock their pipes out against the edge of the table, stand up, unsling their rifles and stroll up to the shooting stand.

I have forgotten all their names. But the faces and manner of shooting of this little local Shooting Guild, I'll never forget. One of them in particular attracted my attention, a sturdy, merry old fellow with a white moustache.

"You manage to keep sufficiently fit and lively for all your sixty summers," I ventured to say to him.

"My dear infant, stick on another eighteen, and you'd be nearer to the mark," he laughed back at me, as he picked up his rifle, and proceeded to score twenty, three times running, every shot slap in the bull!

I was allowed to add my effort, too, and scored seventeen three times running—not too bad for a humble pacifist, who hadn't felt the feel of a rifle in his hand for donkeys' years. The seven Guild Members congratulated me and drank to my health. They also insisted that I should write my name in their Guild Book, and mighty proud I was of it.

Grock the Clown wins praise all the world over. But what of it? I am much more susceptible to my praises being sung as a good citizen. Grock the competent marksman, the excellent man of business, the good-man-at-a-bargain, the irreproachable tax-payer . . . that's the sort of thing I like to hear!

Sixty-nine thousand, three hundred and eighty words! Another six hundred and twenty to go! I must end up now. And I know a good way to end up, by telling what happened to me towards the end of my time in Spain. It was the end of the world on a small scale . . . 'struth, but it was!

Well then, we had finished counting our golden harvest in Almendralejo, had just dismissed our assistants, had a wash and brush-up, and safely stowed our money-bags away beneath the mattress, when a carriage drew up in front of our house and we were called to the window. There in a carriage and pair sat the young Marchese X. and six young ladies, his sisters, in white

frocks and Florentine hats. They had driven
in the previous day from his country estate
in order to be present at the town festivities,
and now wanted us to drive back with them
to N. There we should see, or so they told us,
how a herd of bulls was captured and de-
spatched to Granada for the great bull-fights
there.

We had literally had no sleep for the past
two nights, but the prospect of witnessing
something so unusual, to say nothing of
passing a whole day in the society of such
very attractive ladies, was too much for us.
My performances had already brought me in
touch with the X. family, the charming male
members of which would never fail to call
and see me in my dressing-room in order to
congratulate me in person.

So Antonet and I got into the carriage all
among the dark-eyed beauties, and the
horses started off at a good, brisk pace
through the sombre and shadowy little town
streets, still fresh and cool as the early morning, towards the broiling plains of the open
country.

I have never seen anything like the almost
monstrous strength of the light that beats

down on the southern regions of Spain. There, on a summer morning, you can see neither the earth nor the sky, neither field nor street. You cannot tell where the sky begins and the earth leaves off: the entire world is nothing but one quivering mass of light.

We were accordingly blinded and dazzled, and hardly exchanged a word. A stranger to Spain at the best of times will always feel a certain uneasiness in the presence of Spanish women. The young ladies in question, being daughters of a French mother, were freer and more naturally brought up than most Spanish girls, but even they would show signs, on occasion, of that secret circumspection, that guarded attitude of "touch me not" that makes it so difficult to get to know the women of this country.

We duly arrived at the country seat, and were taken immediately to the Bull Farm where operations were about to begin. The bulls were standing in their enclosure, in the relentless sunshine, dumbly waiting, full of potential energy and mischief. Anybody so much as touching that enclosure, I thought to myself, surely stands every chance of getting a first-rate electric shock. But the whole matter was handled with the utmost calm and expertness. Mounted *vacheros* with long, spiked poles, drove a number of oxen into the enclosure; the bulls obviously sensed that something akin to themselves had arrived; the tameness of their domesticated brethren soon did its work, and one by one the bulls would be attached to them. Then a file of oxen with a bull at the end of it would be driven down a narrow way with high walls on either side. At the end of this narrow way was what looked like a kind of drawbridge leading once more into open country. But no sooner had the last ox crossed this bridge than a wooden partition was smartly shot down between it and the following bull, with another one behind it, so that the bull was made prisoner. This thing that looked like a bridge was nothing less than a truck on low wheels in which the bull could be conveyed to the station and thence on to the goods train.

Seven bulls in turn were treated in this fashion. The eighth was a more difficult proposition, proving amenable neither to the laws of kinship nor crowd psychology. He was a gigantic brute, with smooth skin, darkly glistening, and stood there like a statue in the shadow of an enormous chestnut tree. So huge were his horns they looked like branches.

Nothing would fetch him out, neither coaxing, nor calling nor prodding. Imagine our amazement, as well as our consternation, when Maria, the youngest Marchesa but one, and the boldest and most enterprising of all the sisters, suddenly darted from behind the chestnut tree, and, plucking a red silk handkerchief forth from her white bodice, proceeded to dance around the bull waving the handkerchief to and fro in front of his very nose!

That red flame acted on him like a ton of gunpowder. In a trice the huge beast had lashed himself into a fury and was running with lowered head at the crazy girl who, at the last moment, sprang on one side into safety, while the bull, plunging onwards, entangled his horns in the fencing and was then easily captured. It was this very bull that killed two toreadors a week later in that famous fight in the bull-ring at Granada; the whole of Spain could talk of nothing else for weeks on end afterwards.

This incident had left us all in a high state of excitement. Added to which was the intense heat, together with the animal "tang" that pervaded the bull farm; all this, taken in conjunction with the approved Spanish reserve on the part of the young ladies, and the consequent desire it aroused to overcome it—I must admit that I felt a strong temptation to allow my mind to dwell on other delights than that of the excellent meal now provided for us in the cool inner court of the country house.

Maria of the willowy figure and olive-hued complexion had appealed to me from the start more than any of the other sisters, and I could see I attracted her too, and that's how it happened that we wandered away from the rest of the party, leaving them to sit down to their refreshments while we enjoyed a little, secret rendezvous in the olive orchard on the hill, close by.

So tremendous was the noonday heat that even the grasshoppers had ceased to chirp. A dark cloud, looming up in the distance, foreboded thunder. We strolled together to the top of the hill, then climbed down through the gorse bushes towards cornfields

and up another hill; and all the while the
bold and audacious words I had meant to
say stuck in my gizzard, and I babbled in-
anities like any raw schoolboy in the customary fashion of a man who wants to say
more than he ought and ends by saying nothing at all. Maria was obviously dis-
gruntled, and her silence only made me all
the more embarrassed.

Meanwhile the threatening thundercloud
was looming up rapidly. Spanish thunder-
storms have a way of taking you by surprise,
and when they burst they burst with a vengeance. It was odd that the lightning and
thunder had not already broken from the
clouds bunching so heavily above us. All they
did was to gleam mysteriously, like mother-
of-pearl.

A colossal green grasshopper flew upwards
and into Maria's hair. The young girl put
both her hands up to her head and shook it
like mad.

"Help!" she screamed at me. "Help!"

At last! Bless that grasshopper! Imagine
with what delighted alacrity I plucked the
insect from her hair and no sooner was that
done than courage welled up into me, and I

269

put my arms round her neck in a sort of crazy desperation. She, even crazier than myself, returned the gesture, and then . . . and then . . . oh, I could howl even now, when I think of it—our amorous encounter was cut short by a whole swarm of grasshoppers!

We broke from one another in utter horror, and saw for the first time how the air around us was thick with nothing but grasshoppers. They were descending from the skies in a great black cloud; they covered all the cornfield, they hung in immense clusters from every tree, they crept into every nook and cranny of our clothes, they covered our homeward path with a kind of pulsing, green carpet, and all the time they chirped, and chirped, *and* chirped . . . sirr . . . sirr . . .sirr . . . It was a swarm of African locusts that had settled on the country round!

These predatory, winged creatures proceeded to rain down from the skies, actually obscuring the white, dazzling sunlight that had been beating down upon us; the sun's rays only reached us now, pearl-tinted, through that massive, iridescent cloud. We turned tail and ran, slithering on the green, quivering carpet at our feet, falling into holes that were full of the little pests, and literally wading up to our ankles in the green mass of them.

And still they came . . . and still they came . . .

The olive orchard on the slope of the hill was stripped bare, not an ear of corn could be seen in the cornfield . . . not a blade of wheat . . . not a cob of maize . . . The landscape positively seemed to be shrinking beneath our very eyes: sirrr . . . sirrr . . . sirrr . . . Estremadura was surely being devoured from the earth.

The farm seemed transformed into a mountain of grasshoppers consisting of a mass of wildly waving legs and arms. The insects had found their masters there. Pigs adore eating grasshoppers. They were waltzing in an ecstasy of joy in front of the green heaps, and looking quite green themselves . . .

But Maria of the willowy figure and olive-hued complexion, I never saw again.

32

ADIEU

FROM Westphalia on to Cologne, and thence through Strasbourg to Berne where we put up at the old "Gasthaus" overlooking the Rhone Glacier. Max leaves me, perforce, in the valley to go on up to Geneva where he lives. We have been working together now for more than ten years, infinitely to my own satisfaction, and I think I may say also, to his. Max van Embden is not only an ideal partner, but one of the finest violinists I have ever known, and no record of my doings would be complete that did not contain a thank offering on my part to this good pal of mine, who has done so much to deserve it.

Within another hour I am off again and three hours later am at the frontier town of Chiasso, and speeding in my Isotta Fraschini along the loveliest motor route in the world towards my beloved land of Italy where my home is, on the coast.

As for those seventy thousand words, I have already long over-shot the mark; my typewriter has been typed to a frazzle, and I myself hardly know if I'm on my head or my heels. My brain is tired and my tongue even tireder.

We live in a day that is greedy for the facts of a man's life. They are all on edge to know exactly what happened, when and where it occurred. But what does it all mean—first *this* happened, and then *that* happened . . . so and so . . . and so and so . . . Would it not be both more interesting and more full of significance if something only *might* have happened? But what the world wants it must have. The golden rule of supply and demand, may it prosper! I for one have always obeyed it. So here is the so-called record of my life, guaranteed to be genuine from start to finish, without any extraneous matter. Facts—in fact!

The snow mountains are beginning to glow red, and the shadows deepening in the valley. Sounds of groaning come from the glacier, far away. A block of ice breaks off and thunders down towards the valley. It will be a cool evening. Let's have a Grock, waiter, a double Grock, and damn the expense!

Here I sit, thinking of the little petty existence that is me, and how fortunate I am.

I am Swiss-born. I have three native lands to my credit. I am at home wherever German is spoken and thought. I am at home wherever French is spoken and thought. I am at home wherever Italian is spoken and thought. I am innately incapable of understanding how one nation can hate another or bear a grudge against another. May the devil take all these plague-carrying notions, once for all!

On I go, down by the St. Gotthard towards Italy and Oneglia on the sea-coast where my new house is built. To-morrow morning, when I open my windows, I shall look far, far across the sea towards an island capped with snowy mountains: Corsica!

And how good the heady, red wine is going to taste that is made from my own vines! I shall not only drink it, I shall *bite* it, for the sheer love of it: wine that is good should always be bitten, first. And how good the tomatoes are going to taste, and the vegetable marrows and the sharp tangy green-stuff, and the figs and the almonds and the grapes, and the pomegranates, and the oranges and all and all my very own growing!

I can see myself sitting beneath a tree at a great, round, stone table, with moths, large as bats, with mother-of-pearl wings, fluttering against my lamp. There sits my darling wife, whom I love just as I did when we first met, five and twenty years ago; there sits my dear mother, nearly eighty years old, yet frisky and merry as a five-year-old; there sits my father-in-law with his bald head, an ex-officer of the Carabinieri, still capable of taking to the mountains with his rifle; there sits my mother-in-law, so sturdy and so sound, the proper wife for such a husband; and from the house the strains of a Chopin prelude come drifting, played by my daughter, Bianca, who one of these days will be a great pianist.

So soon as Sunday comes round I shall go and call on you, my dear old Garibbo, my architect and my very good friend, living with your five bachelor sons in your valley of olives and figs; you will have to kill the fatted calf, then, in my honour, and roast every portion of it with your own hands in front of your great fire.

I love my home. Ah, to be home again! Home . . . Home . . . It means such a lot—and I know what it means. Happy the man who can say such a thing.

Yes, indeed, I am a lucky man, a very lucky man. My health is good. I am at peace within myself. I am surrounded by people on whom I can rely, absolutely and entirely.

Enough of these transports of delight. We must break off now, if we don't want the night to overtake us.

Here's to you, with a Double Grock, and much good may it do you—all and every one of you!!!

THE END